Extreme
Revenue Growth

Extreme Revenue Growth

Startup Secrets to Growing Your Sales from $1 Million to $25 Million in Any Industry

VICTOR CHENG

Innovation Press
San Francisco

Copyright © 2010 Victor Cheng
All Rights Reserved

Published by Innovation Press, 548 Market St, #75551, San Francisco, CA 94104

Printed in the United States of America
ISBN: 978-0-9841835-1-7

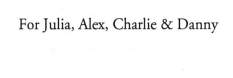

For Julia, Alex, Charlie & Danny

Foreword

For decades, there has been an ongoing fascination with the high-tech industry, a fascination that has grown in recent years with the explosive growth of Internet companies. The interest is usually centered on exciting new products and meteoric rises in stock prices, a recurring theme within the industry.

In my career both inside and outside of technology, I've always found the internal operations of high-tech companies to be much more intriguing than what is usually visible to an outsider—the products, stock price, or headlines.

The innovative ways that CEOs of these fast-growing companies run their businesses are profound and routinely extend beyond being in control of some new technology. These innovations span all facets of the business, from recruiting to management decision making to sales, marketing, and more.

In the pages that follow, there are three things you will notice.

First, this book is intended to be read by CEOs. The perspective taken is the one from the top—seeing how all the pieces of a company fit together.

Second, this book is cross-functional in its nature. It does not describe how your department heads in R&D, sales, marketing, human resources, and operations should run their departments. Instead, it covers how, from the

CEO's perspective, the most important aspects of these departments should interlink and work together. Each department of your company is like a piece of a jigsaw puzzle; you'll find this book focuses a lot on the connection points between the pieces.

Third, I've distilled these management practices into a single cohesive system that can be used by a CEO in any industry. While best known for its great technology breakthroughs, the technology industry has also come up with a number of management breakthroughs.

Anytime you combine the best and brightest talent in the world, the most relentless work ethic you'll see anywhere in the world, and the most venture capital of any industry in the world, you find a ridiculously hypercompetitive environment.

Companies that thrive in this environment are forced, by necessity, to use the growth strategies you'll soon discover. They have no choice. These strategies are essential for survival.

The big opportunity for you is to take these tools and apply them to your industry. I have a favorite saying when it comes to opportunities like this: When you need to use a hammer to get the job done, bring a sledgehammer instead. It's my hope that this book is the sledgehammer you can use in your company to shatter revenue growth barriers and achieve extreme revenue growth.

TABLE OF CONTENTS

INTRODUCTION 2

PART I: CREATING GROWTH 6

1) THE REVENUE GROWTH ENGINE 8

2) THE CUSTOMER: THE PERSON WITH THE MONEY MAKES ALL THE RULES 20

3) MAKE CUSTOMERS A UNIQUE, COMPELLING & CREDIBLE PROMISE 26

4) DISTRIBUTION: THE MOST VALUABLE ASSET OF ALL 44

5) CREATE EASY-TO-SELL PRODUCTS THAT CUSTOMERS LOVE 64

6) THE SUSTAINABLE COMPETITIVE ADVANTAGE 84

PART II: MANAGING GROWTH 92

7) THE 10 TIMES TEST 94

8) STANDARDIZE YOUR OPERATIONS 104

9) EVERY PROBLEM IS A SYSTEMS PROBLEM 114

PART III: SUSTAINING GROWTH 120

10) THE ROLE OF THE CEO 122

11) MANAGING THE GROWTH PORTFOLIO 128

12) TALENT: THE ROCKET FUEL FOR SUSTAINED GROWTH 142

13) ACCOUNTABILITY: THE BREAKFAST OF CHAMPIONS 158

PART IV: HOW TO GET STARTED 166

14) 3 STRATEGIES TO JUMP START GROWTH 168

15) ADDITIONAL RESOURCES 186

About The Author

Victor Cheng serves as a strategic advisor to owners of high-potential growth businesses. He's a former McKinsey consultant and Stanford graduate and has been featured by the Fox Business Network, *TIME* magazine, *Harvard Business Review*, *The Wall Street Journal*, *Fortune Small Business*, and *Inc.* magazine. Victor is also the author of *The Recession-Proof Business* and *Bookmercial Marketing*.

INTRODUCTION

Extreme Revenue Growth

Extreme revenue growth is a direct consequence of making smart decisions, leading a talented team, and keeping everyone focused on getting the right things done. Extreme revenue growth is not an accident; it is the result of deliberate thoughts, behaviors, and actions. Growth is within your control.

You decide which markets you will compete in. You decide which products and services to offer your customers. You decide on which growth engines you'll use to fuel your company's growth. You decide who's on your team. At the end of the day, you decide everything.

The revenue growth your company experiences (or doesn't experience) is a direct consequence of your decisions and actions.

There are three key decisions you need to make to achieve extreme revenue growth:

1) Picking the right growth opportunities to pursue, and picking the right approach for each opportunity,

2) Managing growth by standardizing your operations, and developing business processes that can handle many more customers than you have today, and

3) Sustaining growth by using a disciplined system for managing your growth portfolio, building your team, and maintaining accountability for results.

I need to say that just because something appears to be simple doesn't mean it's necessarily going to be easy to carry out. The devil is very much in the details, and the pages that follow are all about the details—and there are lots of them.

This book describes a unified system for creating, managing, and sustaining extreme revenue growth. Everything in the first chapter is intended to work with everything in the last chapter (and every chapter in between), so I strongly urge you to read this book in the order it was written.

As you read, you'll notice that all the parts of this system fit together. As an example, how you recruit employees is related to which growth opportunities you pursue. The ability of your internal processes to handle dramatic growth is tied to your ability to sustain extreme revenue growth. Your company's annual revenues are directly related to how effective you are in holding your team accountable for results. In short, everything is related to everything else.

In the first section of this book I'll show you how to create revenue growth. You'll discover the foundation of revenue growth: The Revenue Growth Engine. You'll learn about the components of a good revenue growth engine and how they all fit together.

In the second section of this book I'll discuss how to manage the growth once you get it. While this is certainly a nice problem to have, it is still a problem that needs to be addressed. You'll discover several tools for handling these "growing pains" type of challenges.

Finally, in the last section of this book, I'll discuss the keys to sustaining on-going revenue growth. In particular, I'll talk about the role you, as CEO, need to play to sustain growth.

Let's get started by discussing The Revenue Growth Engine—the foundation of all growth.

Part I:
Creating Growth

CHAPTER 1

The Revenue Growth Engine

The foundation of revenue growth in every company is the revenue growth engine. A revenue growth engine is a specific market opportunity combined with your company's approach to capturing it.

A Revenue Growth Engine Consists of Five Key Components:

1) A target customer who's aware of his or her problem.

2) A promise that your company makes to prospective customers.

3) A distribution channel for reaching and transacting with the target customer.

4) A product or service that fulfills the promise made to the customer.

5) A sustainable competitive advantage.

Yes, this seems very basic. You've heard it all before. It sounds like common sense. However, most high-tech companies do not get these key elements right—or if they do get them right once, they cannot sustain their success over the long term.

Be aware that what's required for growth and mastering the subtleties of what's required for growth are two different things. Each can have dramatically different impacts on revenues.

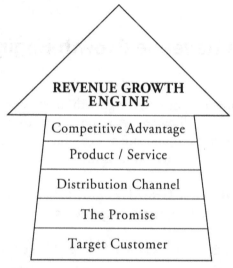

Figure 1-1. The Revenue Growth Engine

For example, while most CEOs are aware of these key issues, many tackle them in the wrong order. Often, they will focus on product development ahead of gaining a thorough understanding of the target customer, determining the right customer promise, and selecting an effective distribution channel. They make this mistake and wonder why their company isn't growing. Again, the details matter.

In this chapter, I'll provide a high-level overview of the key concepts. Once the basics are out of the way I'll use the next few chapters to explain the details—especially the details that usually get screwed-up. I'll also analyze common mistakes and show how to fix them.

The Target Customer

The foundation of a growth engine is a target customer who:

1) has a problem,

2) is aware of this problem, and

3) has the ability and desire to pay (with time or money) to solve this problem.

If there is no problem there is no sale. You can't sell aspirin as a headache remedy to people who never get headaches. You can carry out various market sizing exercises to determine how many people have a particular problem today, and you can engage in market forecasting exercises to predict how many people will likely have the problem in the future. These are all valid things to do, and should be done, but for our purposes you simply need to remember this: No problem, no sale.

The second hurdle is your target customer's level of awareness about his or her problem. Nobody spends money solving a problem they don't even realize they have. Highway 101 runs the length of Silicon Valley in California, and it is littered with companies that crashed and burned trying to solve a problem that their target customer didn't realize they had.

It's twenty times easier to solve a problem people already know they have than to solve a problem they don't realize they have. The reason is financial. If your customers aren't already aware of their problem, you have to invest your marketing resources to teach them about the problem, which leaves you no resources for convincing the customer to buy from your company.

The third hurdle is finding out if the customer cares enough about the problem to pay to solve it. If the customer doesn't care, they won't buy. You can try to make them care, but if, at some fundamental level, they just don't—there's nothing you can do about it. Go find another customer segment to target or a different problem to solve.

You'd be surprised how many startup companies, and startup divisions of larger companies, fail to overcome this basic hurdle. They decide to try to solve a problem the customer *ought* to care about—without appreciating the fact that just because a customer should care doesn't mean they actually do. Again, details matter.

Along these same lines, you must consider whether or not the customer has the money to solve the problem. In business-to-business markets you want to reach people that have a problem and a budget they can tap to solve it.

In cases where the person who has the problem differs from the person with a budget, you have to get both decision makers on board. If you sell a marketing automation system, you will need to find a way to address the concerns of both the VP of Marketing (the person with the problem) and the Chief Information Officer (the person with the technology budget) in the companies you target. If you're not able to do so, you've got an incomplete revenue growth engine opportunity.

On the consumer side, the customer must not only have the money but also the willingness to pay to solve the problem. It's important to note that money is not the only currency a customer spends.

The other currency is time. So if your company is a new media company that gives away a service to one audience (e.g., Google's free search service) and generates revenue indirectly from another source (e.g., Google's Ad Words paid advertising program), you can simply cross out the word "money" in many parts of this book and substitute it with the word "time."

Customers have to pay to play. If they aren't willing to pay with time or money then you're out of luck and will not experience growth.

The Promise:
Make It Unique, Compelling, and Credible

The second component of a revenue growth engine is the promise you make to customers to get them to buy. This component is frequently overlooked or its importance grossly under-estimated. The way to get a customer to buy is to offer a promise that is different (or at least different enough) from the competition and one that provides a genuinely compelling benefit. In addition, this promise must be credible.

The promise is what gets the customer to buy. Most people (especially engineers) find this idea troublesome and are conflicted by it. Don't customers buy because of the product or service? At the end of the day, a customer doesn't really want nor need a particular product or service; they only buy based on the *promise* of how they'll benefit from the product or service.

For example, nobody buys an electric drill because they want one—they want perfectly sized holes and buy the electric drill on the promise that the product will deliver the outcome they want.

The Chief Information Officer (CIO) who invests in a million dollar enterprise software system is not buying the software because she likes it; she's buying it because she needs to get her manufacturing cycle times down by 25%. The truth is, she won't know if the product can really deliver until many months after the purchase. So, she buys on the promise of a future benefit.

I'm fond of saying: "The role of the promise is to get customers to buy. The role of the product is to keep the customer happy after the sale and to keep you from being called a liar."

This is the underlying reason why an inferior product will often outsell a superior one (much to the frustration of the engineers who created it). Customers often don't know the difference between two products unless they buy and use both. Since most customers only buy one product, they never experience for themselves which one is better. Instead, **they simply choose whichever company offers a more compelling benefit or a more credible promise**.

Distribution Channel:
Unless You Can Reach a Customer,
Everything Else Is Irrelevant

Once you have a target customer in mind, and have found a promise that works, you're ready for the next step in creating a revenue growth engine. You need to find or create one or more distribution channels that you can use to reach your target customer.

How you intend to distribute a product or service needs to be determined (or at least considered) prior to product/service development. You will likely need to modify your product to make it more compatible with your chosen distribution channel (i.e., resellers, retail stores, enterprise sales force, value-added resellers, search engine advertising, or the Internet).

Here is a simple example: Let's assume you sell a software product that can be bought as packaged software or purchased on a hosted subscription basis. You can sell this offering in a number of ways. You could sell it using a field sales force, through a telephone sales force, or you could sell entirely over the Internet using a free-trial model. If you intend to use remote or self-service selling, you'd want to make sure your software works through corporate firewalls. However, if you were selling and installing the software inside the corporate firewall, this feature would not be important.

Another example comes from a company I encountered many years ago, when it was on its last breath before crashing and burning. It had been in business for four years. In about 20 minutes, I was able to determine how they screwed-up their company and burned through tens of millions in venture money.

In short, they built their product before they figured out their distribution channel. They ended up building a very useful product that they could not deliver to their target customer.

To protect their identity I'll keep the specifics vague. They sold an enterprise software system that was meant to be an add-on to a much larger system implementation along the lines of an SAP, Oracle, or other ERP system. Their product was radically better than their competitors. Unlike their competitor's product, their product didn't require extensive custom coding; you could literally install it and get it working almost immediately. And, if that wasn't enough, the product sold for 80% less than the competition.

To most people, this would appear to be a slam-dunk opportunity: An 80% lower price, genuine product superiority, and a price-to-performance ratio that was unmatched by any other competitor. So what went wrong? In a nutshell—distribution.

Large ERP-type implementations are controlled by the large IT consulting firms, like Accenture. Because of this fact, the startup company attempted to partner with these system integrators. Unfortunately, they never succeeded in getting the attention of those companies.

System integrators are interested in selling integration services. This product was too easy to install and didn't offer the integrator any opportunities to generate service revenue.

A system integrator would actually lose money by recommending it to clients, instead of the product they would normally recommend. Not surprisingly, the company had no luck selling to, or through, system integrators.

They also tried to build an enterprise sales force to sell directly to enterprise accounts. They encountered two problems:

First, they had difficulty recruiting seasoned commission-oriented sales professionals because their average selling price was a small five-figure investment (the top sales people wanted to sell six, seven, and eight-figure deals).

Second, the customers themselves didn't want to deviate from the recommended solution provided by the system integrator. Because the product was such a small piece of the overall system, it simply wasn't important enough to the customer to create risk in the rest of the project to accommodate this add-on functionality.

In the end the company crashed and burned, in spite of having a better product. They designed a product that wasn't compatible with the distribution channels they attempted to use. As a rule of thumb, you can't just build an easy-to-use product. You must also deliberately engineer your product so that it will be easy to sell through the distribution channel you select. It's a small, but vital, detail.

The Product or Service

Now it's time to create a product or service. Once a customer buys on the promise of a major benefit, it's the role of the product to deliver on that promise and to create a happy customer.

In the revenue growth engine creation process, the product development step occurs late in the process for a deliberate reason. The product must be designed to meet the promises made to customers that generate revenues and to be compatible with the distribution channel needed to reach the customer.

If you start the product development process too early, you don't yet know which promises customers are willing to pay for and which distribution channel factors you need to consider.

This is a significant departure from how product development is approached in many high-tech companies. In these companies, you'll hear a lot about features and specifications. In most cases, these requirements have to do with how the product will be used by the end user. My argument is that engineering efforts should include meeting the requirements of the selling process and not just the product usage process.

Sustainable Competitive Advantage

Creating revenue growth doesn't always mean you can sustain that growth. Generating extreme revenue growth has a habit of getting the attention of prospective competitors, and it encourages them to come and compete with you.

The lifespan of a revenue growth engine depends entirely on what competitive advantages your company possesses and uses in conjunction with that particular growth engine. A competitive advantage is a physical or intangible asset that gives you an advantage over the competition.

A physical asset might be having the largest sales force, distribution network, or satellite office network in your industry. Intangible assets are things like a key patent, brand reputation, or an exclusive partnership with a much larger company.

The more difficult an advantage is for a competitor to duplicate, the more sustainable the advantage. By deliberately linking a growth engine to one or more competitive advantages, you'll be able to sustain revenues from that engine for a longer period of time.

Creating a New Growth Engine with Minimal Effort

When you put these five ingredients together in a business—a target customer, a promise, a distribution channel, a product, and a sustainable competitive advantage—you have a growth engine. Some CEOs in the product-centric high-tech world tend to equate revenue growth opportunities with a product development project. The only problem with that approach is that it leaves so much money on the table.

Often, it's much easier to make simple adjustments—to your target customer, to your promise, or to your distribution channel—than it is to change your product. I'll use a consumer packaged goods example to illustrate this point. Several years ago, heart disease researchers discovered that taking a baby aspirin every day could significantly reduce chances of a heart attack (this is, of course, not medical advice—you should seek the advice of a medical professional prior to ingesting any medications).

Armed with this knowledge, Bayer decided to create a growth engine to capitalize on this opportunity. They decided to target consumers concerned about their heart attack risk. This wasn't the same audience as those concerned about getting rid of headaches. So the first step taken in creating this new growth engine involved targeting a different type of customer.

Their next step was to make a new type of promise in their advertising and on their product label. They promised that taking a low-dose aspirin every day could reduce the risk of a heart attack.

Distribution wasn't a key concern because Bayer knew they could leverage their existing retailer relationships to get a "prevent heart attacks" offering on the shelves, giving them a competitive advantage.

Next, they introduced a low-dosage aspirin they described as the "exact same dosage" used in the clinical research that demonstrated that a small dose of aspirin every day reduced the chance of heart attacks. In reality, all they did was take the baby aspirin product and change the label to support this new promise. No new research and development work was required.

In manufacturing, they used the same line that made the baby aspirin product. The only difference was in the very last step of the manufacturing process. They simply changed the label on the product to one that would feature the new promise.

Even though the original research on using aspirin to prevent heart attacks was first published in 1989, Bayer's "low dose" product continues to appear on shelves decades later. If the shelf space this product gets in my local supermarket is any indication, this "low dose" product generates a significant portion of Bayer's revenue in the aspirin category. That's pretty impressive revenues from just changing a label isn't it?

This example illustrates that by simply tweaking one or more of the five growth engine components, you can create a new growth engine for your company.

In the next few chapters I'll go through the common problems found in each component of a growth engine, and will discuss suggested solutions.

Key Ideas:

- All revenue growth starts with the target customer, who has a problem

- To get a customer to buy you must make them a promise that is unique, credible and compelling

- Distribution is critical because, without it, your prospects will never see your product

- Design products to be easy to sell (i.e., compatible with your distribution channel) and to fulfill expectations set with the customer

- The lifespan of your revenue growth engine depends on the sustainability of your competitive advantage

CHAPTER 2

The Customer: The Person With The Money Makes All The Rules

The first step in creating a revenue growth engine is simple. Start with the person who has the money: the customer. Figure out what the customer wants, but is not getting elsewhere, and give it to him or her.

However, just because something is simple does not always mean it is easy to do.

In this chapter we will examine the common problems related to identifying and knowing your target customer and will use real world examples to learn how to tackle these challenges.

All of the problems listed in the troubleshooting section of this, and subsequent, chapters result in a common, highly visible symptom: No revenue growth.

While the lack of revenue growth is a single, visible symptom, it has dozens of potential causes.

A small sample of the most common problems, and their solutions, is listed in this chapter and throughout the remainder of the book.

Target Customer Problem #1:
You're Guessing (Incorrectly) About
What the Target Customer Wants

A common problem that occurs in startup companies, and in startup divisions of larger companies, is that the company does not have a clear understanding of the target customer.

I have a simple acid test that I use to determine how well an organization knows their target customer: I ask them to give me the first and last names of all the people that best represent their target customer.

You'd be surprised how often I am unable to get the first and last name of a single person. I use this test because the attempt to create a new growth engine is often based on incorrect information.

If you don't have accurate information about what you're aiming for, you can't possibly hit the target. Here's the key to getting accurate information about target customers: Talk to them.

One of my clients is the CEO of a $20 million dollar a year e-commerce business. I once asked this client: "What's the number one problem your customers have that causes them to spend $20 million a year with you?" He jotted down his answer.

At my urging, he surveyed and interviewed his customers over the next two weeks only to discover that his answer was number five on the customers' list of problems.

His reaction, when he discovered this information, was: "You mean I've built a $20 million a year business completely missing the fact of what's important to my customers? I shouldn't be at $20 million. By now, I should be, at least, at $50 million."

While the company had achieved what would be considered a respectable level of revenues, it had not maximized its revenue potential. It pays better to know what your target customers want, than to guess.

Target Customer Problem #2:
Customer Doesn't Want to Buy
What You Want to Sell

Another very common problem is that the target customer doesn't want to buy what you want to sell. Ironically, this really isn't a target customer problem—it's your company's problem.

At the end of the day, you can't make your customers want something they fundamentally do not want or need. When there is an underlying desire, you can use sales and marketing to sharpen demand and increase the customer's sense of urgency for solving their problems. But, no matter how savvy you are, you cannot make customers want something they just don't care about.

There's a saying: "A great sales person can sell ice to Eskimos." I'm fond of saying: "A great marketer (or marketing-savvy CEO) realizes it's more productive to sell space heaters to Eskimos than ice."

Ask yourself if you currently have growth engines in your portfolio that are metaphorically attempting to sell ice to Eskimos.

Remember, companies exist to supply products and services that customers demand. Unfortunately, it does not work so well when you try to supply products and services you hope customers will demand.

Target Customer Problem #3:
Customer Has a Problem, But Not a Severe Problem

Sometimes a target customer has the problem you thought they did, but the problem is not severe; the target customer has no sense of urgency with regards to solving the problem.

This is a tougher case because you have to make an assessment as to whether the urgency is likely to increase (e.g., the "Year 2000" computer problem was not urgent in 1995 but was very urgent in 1999) or if the problem is fundamentally not that important to the customer.

If the customer's problem will forever be modest in nature, this caps the revenue potential of the growth engine you're considering. What you decide to do next is somewhat dependent on the other growth engines you have in your portfolio, their maturity level, and the resources required by each one. Generally speaking, I would suggest that you start looking for alternative growth opportunities.

Target Customer Problem #4:
Not Recognizing That Adjacent Customer Segments
Are Growing Faster Than the One
You're Currently Targeting

Most markets are fairly dynamic and continually evolving, and it's often difficult to spot the completely hidden growth opportunity. You must not only see it before anyone else does, you must also capture it ahead of the market. People do it, but it's tough.

Equally important, but much easier, is recognizing when a competitor has successfully tapped into a new customer segment adjacent to the one you're targeting.

An example of this comes from the personal computer (PC) industry. Many PC manufacturers did not recognize the early trend of previous desktop PC buyers replacing their desktops with notebook PCs. These buyers were not the "road warriors" traditionally targeted by notebook PC manufacturers but, rather, the occasional PC user who wanted the option of mobility.

Many years ago in the airline industry, competitors failed to recognize how Southwest Airlines had built an entire business by going after customers who had been driving to their destination by car, rather than flying. It was a fast growing segment missed by the other airlines—until many years later.

Here's the lesson: You must pay attention to your competitor's growth engines—particularly the ones that work—as a way to identify potential growth opportunities for your company.

Target Customer Problem #5:
Not Recognizing That Your Existing Customers May Be Different From the Newer Customers You Want to Target

For companies that have been around a while, you'll often find that buyers of legacy products aren't always the same buyers of future products. It's important to keep the two distinct, particularly if your company has gone through some major product evolutions.

An example of this is realizing that your legacy mainframe software buyers may not be the same buyers for your client server software. Or, a more recent version of this is recognizing that your client server software buyers might not be the buyers of browser-based client applications.

Here's the general rule: Yesterday's target customer may not be tomorrow's target customer.

Closing Thoughts

All target customer problems discussed in this chapter result from not knowing the customer well enough or not realizing that a new type of customer is emerging. At the end of the day, the customer is the foundation of all successful businesses, so you need to think about them early and often.

Key Ideas:

- All revenue growth opportunities start with getting to know the person with the money—the customer

- You can't make your customers want something they don't want or need

- Adjust your target customer over time to adapt to changing markets and to create new opportunities

CHAPTER 3

Make Customers A Unique, Compelling & Credible Promise

After selecting a target customer, the second step is to determine what promise you'll make to get them to buy. The ideal promise is one that is unique, compelling, and credible.

There's a reason why each of these steps is essential: If your promise is not unique there is no incentive for a customer to pick your company over any other competitor. If a legitimate difference does exist between you and your competitors' promises, your promise should clearly indicate that difference. Otherwise, there is no differentiation in the mind of the customer.

Actual product differences matter only if they help you differentiate the promise you make to your customers. This is a subtle but vital distinction.

This leads to our second point. Customers don't buy products; they buy what a product does for them. In other words, customers buy based on their perception of how a product will benefit them. Your promise must offer a compelling benefit. If the promise is not compelling, you are, in effect, promising to solve a problem your customer doesn't really care about.

Finally, you need to make your promise credible. In many markets buyers are extremely skeptical. They assume all vendors are liars (or at least exaggerators). When you combine this skepticism with the common complaint that "all those companies sound the same," buyers don't know who to buy from and end up choosing randomly.

There are several key problems that arise when developing a unique, compelling, and credible promise. Let's look at the most common problems and your options for addressing them.

Problem #1:
Your Promise Is Not Unique (or Not Unique Enough) Compared to Your Competition

This is probably the number one problem I see in high-tech companies, and here's why knowing about it is so important.

Providing a dramatically different promise, even if your product is similar to the products offered by your competition, forces the customer to consider what you're offering in more detail.

If your promise sounds the same as your competitors' promises, your offer gets lumped together with your competitors' offers. There are numerous tools at your disposal for making your promise unique. There's absolutely no excuse for failing to improve the differentiation of your promise in your marketplace.

Consider Promising the Polar Opposite of What the Competition Is Promising

If the rest of the pack promises the lowest prices consider promising the highest price in the industry—and then figure out what the heck you have to include in your product to justify the higher price.

If the rest of your industry promises customers the most comprehensive features in town, consider promising "just the features you need." Your promise then becomes: "Solving your problem with simplicity."

If the rest of the competition promises the fastest system setup time in the industry, consider promising the slowest (but 200% more thorough) setup process in the industry.

This technique is based on the "Zig-Zag" principle. If everyone else decides to "zig," then you consider "zagging" instead. Of course, you will need to carefully consider this strategy before employing it—sometimes it makes sense and at other times it doesn't. However, here's the general rule of thumb: Any time there's an opportunity to be the polar opposite of your competition it's worth taking a hard look to see if it makes sense.

Be Number One in Your Industry at Something, Even if It Means Being Mediocre at Everything Else

In a cluttered marketplace there's no benefit to being the same as everyone else. If everyone else offers average quality and average service at an average price, you're much better off picking one of the three in which to lead your industry. This means that you must also be willing to risk sacrificing the other elements of your promise.

You are better off being the company offering the highest quality in town, but with absolutely no service, and at the highest prices, than offering something middle of the road. You will certainly alienate a large portion of your market but will attract a narrower segment that values quality more than anything else.

The idea here is that you have to be dramatically better than your competition—at something—to warrant the attention of prospective buyers. A related rule of thumb is that it's good to be either loved or hated because "there ain't no money in the middle."

Solve a Bigger Problem

When a CEO is struggling for ideas to make a promise more unique I can always rely on the strategy of solving a bigger problem, because it works in any market situation. The gist of this strategy is to solve a problem that is bigger than what your industry is accustomed to solving on behalf of customers.

By expanding the problem to be solved you instantly open up ways to distinguish your promise in your marketplace. Let's look at several technology and non-technology examples to drill this point home.

In the portable music player market all the hardware manufacturers were slugging it out over who could build the better, cheaper, cooler-looking MP3 player. Apple had its iPod device, which did indeed look cool. However, it was Apple's brilliant strategic decision to "solve a bigger problem" that really skyrocketed sales.

Apple introduced their iTunes digital music download service that works well only with iPod devices. Apple realized that people did not really want to buy portable music players (the product); they wanted to enjoy portable music. It's a subtle, but major, distinction. Apple solved the bigger problem and left their competitors in the dust.

The underlying technique for solving a bigger problem involves two simple steps: First, look at the things the customer purchases before and after they buy your product; and second, look at the activities the customer engages in before and after they buy your product. Using this "before and after" analysis, you can identify all the possible options for "solving a bigger problem."

In the Apple example, they realized that after customers bought a portable music player from Apple, or anyone else, they still had a lot of work to do before they could actually enjoy portable music. A customer had to get into the cars and navigate traffic to get to a mall. Once there, she had to find the music store, pick out a new compact disc (CD), wait in line, pay the cashier, and sign the credit card slip.

From there, it was back to the car to navigate traffic home, and then park and lock the car. Once inside the house they would lock the door, turn on the computer, wait for it to boot up, and open up the music player console. She still had to open the CD packaging, put the CD in the computer's CD player, "rip" or load the music onto the computer, transfer the music to the portable player, and then hit the play button.

Just the act of writing these steps is laborious. Shouldn't it have been blatantly obvious to all the portable music player manufacturers what a miserable experience that was for the customer?

Unfortunately, the other companies missed it because they defined the customer's problem as a hardware problem. By focusing on this narrow definition of the problem, they missed the opportunity to solve a bigger chunk of the customer's larger problem.

While the Apple example involved a major shift of industry boundaries, there are much simpler examples that follow the same "solve a bigger problem" idea.

Let's say your company manufactures laser printers. An example of "solving a bigger problem" would be to include six months' worth of consumables (e.g., laser toner cartridges) with the printer. You instantly shift your customer promise from delivering a "quality laser printer" (the same promise as your competitors) to delivering 25,000 laser printed pages without any hassles of running out of or having to re-order toner. This immediately sets you apart from your competition.

To solve an even bigger problem, you could offer your customers a free 90-day "toner replenishment" subscription that automatically rolls them into a monthly auto-ship replenishment program.

This solves the customer's headache of having to continually re-order toner. Remember, customers don't want laser printers; they want nice looking pages for life. If you're in the laser printer business, you tend to think very narrowly about the problem. If you're in the "nice looking pages for life" business, you realize that your customers are going to have to re-order toner dozens of times over the next 10 years. Why not solve the customer's "bigger problem" from the outset, with a single purchasing decision?

Would such a promise work? I have no idea—you'd have to test it. However, I do know that it's a unique promise with a compelling benefit. Because of this uniqueness, customers will pay more attention to it than if you make the same promise everyone else is making.

Regardless of whether a customer loves or hates a unique promise they are forced to stop and consider it; they can't simply continue with their autopilot mentality that rejects all vendors because they seem to be completely identical.

Solve a Bigger Problem by Bundling Third-Party Products with Yours

What happens if you don't have the staff to support "free" services with your product, or you don't have product development capacity for creating add-on products, or even additional features?

In these situations you can still "solve a bigger problem" by pre-bundling the commonly used accessories customers typically buy with your product. Even if you buy these third-party products at retail prices, the simple convenience of a single package will be appealing to your customers.

This approach is like the difference between selling a digital camera and selling a digital camera kit. A kit includes the lens, carrying case, protective lens filters, the appropriate type of memory card, and the right cable to connect to the computer. This solves a "bigger problem" for the customer—eliminating the need to evaluate other products in related categories and to research compatibility issues. It's all done for them.

In the enterprise hardware and software markets vendors sell "solution sets" that are often joint-marketed by alliance partners. Pre-bundling is based on the same idea. Instead of promising the customer only the benefits of your component, you can promise the benefits of the entire solution set. You can do this even if the other components of the solution come from other suppliers.

Niche the Promise to a
More Targeted Customer

Another technique for beefing up the uniqueness of your promise is to target the promise to a more focused audience. For example, if you sell an accounting system, simply add the words "for dentists" or "for attorneys" to your promotional materials.

If you sell noise-canceling headphones for aircraft pilots, you can add the words "for jet pilots" or "for commuter plane pilots."

You can validate the promise with an argument that different types of aircraft generate different types of noise, and the headsets are specially designed for your target customer's needs.

Intuit has started using this technique over the past few years with their QuickBooks product. Interestingly, they offered a "one size fits all" single edition of QuickBooks for many years, before deciding to create industry-specific versions.

During the time period when they only offered a single version of QuickBooks, they were vulnerable to any competitor who was willing to niche a competitive product to the specific needs of a niche audience.

Sometimes, creating a niche version of a product only requires superficial changes. Often, much of the niche-specific differentiation can come from training programs, services, or other non-engineering related deliverables.

Multi-Niche the Promise to
Multiple Targeted Customers

The niche strategy is not just a technique relegated to smaller companies. Large companies can use the same technique—with a twist. Instead of targeting a single niche, you can multi-niche your products by targeting multiple niches. You would simply have multiple "editions" of your product that would enable you to make the promise that "this edition was made specifically with your needs in mind."

You could create dozens of editions, with perhaps minor (or no) differences in features, that would support making more specialized promises.

For some people this may seem a bit sneaky or devious. Allow me to explain why this is not the case and, in fact, is a significant customer benefit in both perception and reality.

Let's go back to the accounting software example. For the general accounting package, you promise to "keep track of your customer's purchasing history." For the dentist edition, you make a more specific promise—to keep track of "patient" billing history. For the attorney edition, you promise to keep track of "client" billings.

At first this just seems like word play. In reality, the words make a difference to the customer. A dentist may equate "customer" with product sales.

Thus, a dentist might assume that keeping track of "customer purchasing history" has to do with the selling of physical goods and not services. However, when you mention "patient billing history," the dentist knows the product will work for him.

Even if your product functionally serves a wide range of users, customers don't know that. They will assume that a more specialized offering is better, more relevant, and more appropriate for them than a generic offering. More importantly, they leap to this conclusion quickly and with less comparison-shopping than if they were considering a generic product.

Problem #2:
Your Promise Offers No Compelling Benefit

If your promise offers a benefit the target customer doesn't find compelling, this means you don't know your target customer well enough. You can refer back to Chapter 2 for assistance with understanding the target customer.

You have two options here: You can keep the same target customer and find the benefit they do care about (then change your product to support the new promise); or you can change the target customer to one that values the promise you're already making (and keep the promise that your product is already able to back up).

Either way, the general rule of thumb here is: If you find yourself in the situation of promising the wrong benefit, back up and learn more about your target customer before trying again.

Problem #3:
Your Promise Is Unique and Compelling, but Your Target Customer Doesn't Believe You

What if your promise is unique, and you're certain the offer is compelling, but sales are still down? This often means prospective customers don't believe your promise. Skepticism among consumers and business-to-business customers is probably at an all-time high, while trust is at an all-time low.

To illustrate this point take a stack of 100 one-dollar bills and try to give them away, one at a time, to people on the street.

You will find it's surprisingly difficult. I did this once as an experiment with a colleague in downtown Palo Alto, California. After nearly thirty attempts we had not given away a single one-dollar bill. In fact, when we walked up to people with the one-dollar bill in hand, arm extended (as if to hand it to them), the people being approached would immediately start walking away. We didn't even get a chance to offer them free money.

We had a unique promise, with a compelling benefit, right? The problem was people were so skeptical they didn't believe the promise. Instead, they thought there had to be a catch and did not believe anything we had to say.

Your target customer is the same. He doesn't trust you or your competitors. He assumes you are lying or at least exaggerating your promises.

In fact, companies that exaggerate their promises ("We're the best in the industry" or "We're number one") is such a common practice that it's actually acknowledged by U.S. law.

As I understand it, a company making a general boast that they're the best is called "puffery"—and it's legal. The lawmakers determined that since everyone knows companies exaggerate and nobody believes them anyway, there's no harm in letting companies exaggerate their non-numerical claims (of course this is not legal advice— please seek legal counsel prior to making claims of any type). That's a pretty sad commentary on the state of skepticism, particularly in the United States.

So how do you counter such skepticism? You must supply overwhelming proof that what you say is true. I'll list several ways you can provide this proof. At the end of the day, it is simply impossible to have too much proof.

Proof Technique #1:
Testimonials and Customer References

Hands down, the best way to provide proof to skeptical customers is to provide them with customer testimonials. Show them letters and notes from your happy customers. Let them watch video clips of your customers explaining how happy they are with your products and services. Invite them to attend a live, in-person event to meet your happy customers.

This works equally well selling to consumers as it does to other businesses. When I ran a division of an enterprise software company the best introductory marketing piece I ever created was a nice-looking, leather-bound case studies book. The book included two-page profiles of nearly 30 of our Fortune 500 clients and included detailed talking points.

It provided specifics—such as the first and last name of individuals we dealt with—and details about their situations and concerns.

It also included information on which products they purchased, and statements regarding "before" and "after" financial results that demonstrated the benefits of using our products.

This case studies book replaced the standard "Company Overview" PowerPoint presentation used prior to my involvement (and that is used pretty much by every other enterprise-oriented vendor out there).

The reason it worked so well is that it provided ample proof that the most respected and well-known Fortune 500 companies trusted our solution. We didn't have to say we were the best in our market, our proof made the point for us.

Proof Technique #2:
Demonstrations and Free Trials

Another way to prove your point is with a simple demonstration. Simply demo your product to a customer or allow them to try it out for themselves. Demos work incredibly well at proving your point. If your product is easy to use, demonstrate the product and prove it. Better yet, let your customers try the products themselves so they discover first-hand how easy it is to use.

Here's an interesting story that illustrates this point. At one time in my career I was interim CIO of a fast-growing company about to go public. I had a $1 million dollar information technology budget, and had to implement an enterprise level accounting, sales force automation, customer service, and human resources system.

On two consecutive days I had two different vendors come in to demo their products. One vendor came in with one sales person and a sales engineer. I gave the sales engineer 15 minutes to demonstrate 17 specific things I wanted to see before I would kick him out of my office. The guy was understandably nervous, talked a mile a minute, but did all 17 things very quickly. I ended up giving him a much longer meeting and invited him to come back to show me more. His initial demo certainly proved his argument that his product could meet my needs and that it was easy to use.

On the next day the sales team from a well-known software company came in to present a system similar to the one I'd seen the previous day. However, this well-known company brought in nine people to demo their product. (So much for backing up the claim that their product was easy to use.) If it were that easy, why did they need nine people to demo it?

I had a member of my staff kick off the meeting. I stepped in a few minutes late and said to the sales engineer who was demonstrating the accounting module, "Show me how my assistant could use the system to issue a purchase order for a $1 pencil." (As you can tell by now, I'm big on simple acid tests.)

After 23 minutes of trying, the sales engineer could not fulfill this simple request. I remember thinking, "If nine people can't demonstrate how to order a $1 item in this accounting system in 23 minutes, how in the world are my users going to be able to do it?" I walked out of the meeting a few minutes later and let my staff sit through the rest of the meeting. As you might have guessed, I did not buy.

Bottom line: If your product really works, demo it. And if it doesn't, by all means, create one that does.

Incidentally, there is a good reason for working on the "promise" component of the growth engine prior to product development. Sometimes you will want to create product features that boost the "demo-ability" of your product, even if end users will not use them very often.

At one time I marketed and sold an enterprise software system that was used by both technical and business users. The strength of the product was that it had an extraordinary level of configurability and flexibility for the technical user.

Unfortunately, the first few versions of this product did not include anything visual that could be demonstrated to business people. I remember making a comment to the engineering team: "Guys, I cannot demo APIs to a business user; I've got to have something visual to show them or they won't believe a word I tell them."

This is why figuring out the promise, and how to make it credible, comes first in the growth engine creation process. The promise you decide to make has implications for how you approach product development, and needs to be considered before the product is developed.

Proof Technique #3:
Increase the Specificity of Your Proof

Here's a simple way to increase the credibility of your proof. Simply increase the specificity of the proof. Let's go back to the case studies book I created as a marketing tool for a business-to-business sales force. I trained our sales people to memorize and mention the first and last name of the lead contact for each account in the case studies book. I did this for an important reason: Specific details improve the credibility of the story.

In addition, I deliberately did not print those names on the actual hard copy version of the book show to prospective customers. I had a separate talking points guide that the sales person needed to memorize. I did this to improve the credibility of the sales person. Being able to rattle off key points from a case study created the impression that the sales representative was intimately familiar with each of these accounts. It improved the sales representative's stature as a bona fide expert and gave them more respect inside the account. Specifics increase credibility.

Here's another example: Since a lot of my client work involves integrating marketing strategies with the rest of a client's operations I'm familiar with a number of vendors in the marketing field. One such company is InfoUSA. They happen to be one of the largest, if not the largest, mailing list companies in the United States.

InfoUSA has armies of people doing data entry. They enter every single yellow pages and white pages entry from every phone book in America. They also have an army of people calling every phone number, every year, to verify its accuracy. But until they made one change recently most of their small- and medium-size business customers did not appreciate the enormous presence InfoUSA has in the mailing list industry.

I was pleased to see the following addition at the top of their Web site: "A $750 million a year public company with 4 million customers." It sure beats their former slogan "Sales Solutions Since 1972." I also noticed that every year they update the revenue number and customer count. It's a very smart thing to do, and I'd bet that if they scientifically compared their Web site sales with, and without, that single sentence, you'd see a noticeable difference in revenues. Specificity increases credibility and credibility increases sales.

Key Ideas:

- They key to driving sales is to present customers with a unique, credible promise that includes a compelling benefit

- There are several ways to differentiate your company from your competitors: offer the polar opposite of what the competition is offering ("zig" when others "zag"); be #1 in your industry at something, even if you have to be dead last at everything else; solve a bigger or broader problem than your competitors are accustomed to solving; or focus on a narrower customer segment than your competitors are willing to focus on

- A more unique, more compelling, promise only drives more sales if the promise is credible. To boost the credibility of your promise provide overwhelming proof that what you say is true through customer testimonials, product demos, free trials—and provide highly specific details to boost the credibility of your promise

CHAPTER 4

Distribution: The Most Valuable Asset of All

Distribution (the ability to communicate and transact with a customer) is consistently the most underestimated factor and missed opportunity in most tech- and Internet-based companies. I'll even argue that distribution is more important than product development. If you have good distribution there will be an endless line of companies wanting to partner with you to take advantage of it. The opposite, however, is much less common.

Wal-mart doesn't manufacture a single product. It is, however, the single largest distribution channel for consumer packaged goods in the world. They have direct access to more customers, more easily, than any other company in the world.

Intuit has an enormous distribution channel through its retail, online, and wholesaling partners. Through these extensive relationships Intuit has no trouble introducing new products into these channels.

In addition, recognizing the importance of controlling distribution, Intuit has made extensive efforts to market directly to customers—bypassing third-party distribution channels. Through their online store, downloadable software, and hosted versions of all its key products, they are building direct relationships with customers on an increasingly large scale. It's all about distribution—because without it you can't sell a darn thing.

The same is true in business-to-business markets. The large Enterprise Resource Planning (ERP) companies, like SAP, dominate because of their massive, installed base of customers. On-going relationships with these customers allow SAP to communicate with those customers with ease and at low cost. In short, they have distribution.

When a company like SAP wants to introduce a proprietary or third-party product they can reach a surprisingly high percentage of the CIOs of the Fortune 500 in less than 45 days. That's the power of distribution.

In the online world, Amazon, eBay and GoDaddy have enormous distribution power and reach. These companies have prospered, in part, because their CEOs recognized that they're really in the business of distribution.

Over the past few years Amazon.com has added category after category of products to their Web site; providing more products for their existing customers to buy. (Incidentally, this is precisely what you do when you have strong distribution; you cram as many high-quality, relevant products and services as possible through your distribution system.) Amazon has capitalized on their distribution system extremely well.

The auction site eBay has done the same. In addition to introducing an ever-increasing array of transactional services to its members (eBay Stores, PayPal, escrow services), eBay has continually worked to grow its distribution—particularly internationally.

GoDaddy has come to dominate the domain registrar business mostly because they realized they're not actually in the domain registrar business at all—they're in the distribution business. If you register a domain name on GoDaddy you will be provided with an almost comical number of up-sells and cross-sells. You'll be offered Web hosting services, a blog service, advanced e-mail accounts, Web site marketing services, privacy services, deluxe privacy services, and the list goes on and on and on. Really! But hey, they "get it." They're in a distribution business that happens to involve registering domain names.

One of the reasons distribution is such an enormous asset is because of the economics of distribution. Here's how it works. Acquiring a first-time customer is expensive. If you're like most companies, 80% of your sales and marketing resources get consumed while trying to acquire new customers. These customers don't know you, don't trust you, and can't tell you apart from your competitors.

To get your message across you need to blitz them with your message. Call them on the phone, put sales people on airplanes, whatever it takes. In contrast, you could pick up the phone or send an e-mail to your best customers to let them know about a new product and get an order within minutes or a few weeks—depending on the nature of your business.

So in the distribution game selling to a new customer is the least profitable part of the business. It's necessary, but not nearly as profitable as selling more to existing customers. The companies that are smart with distribution recognize this and are extremely focused on selling more to existing customers.

Dominate New Customer Acquisition by Selling More to Existing Customers

To dominate the war for new customers the single, biggest, most unstoppable advantage is a superior ability to sell more to existing customers. This linkage isn't initially obvious, but if you fully appreciate this relationship, you will never look at your business in the same way again.

When a company does a good job selling to existing customers they can afford to spend more money to acquire new customers. Taken to the extreme, this simple mathematical relationship has enormous strategic and competitive implications. If you can lead the industry in sales to existing customers you will have the largest marketing war chest in your industry, bar none. This isn't marketing theory; it's a mathematical fact.

Here's a simple example: Let's say you're trying to sell to a Fortune 500 account and are competing against a big company like SAP. Let's also assume that the typical SAP account spends $15 million with SAP over 5 years. In contrast, your typical customer spends only $100,000 over the same time period.

The way the math works is SAP can afford to invest $14,999,999 to secure that account and still make a $1 profit, whereas you can only afford to spend $99,999 to secure the same account. In that situation, who is going to win?

When you're at a 150:1 marketing investment disadvantage it's very tough to come out ahead. Once again, this illustrates the power and importance of distribution.

Distribution is hands down one of the most important aspects of creating a revenue growth engine. It is also the factor that is consistently underestimated and is often considered only as an afterthought to product development.

Among many high-tech startups the mentality is: "Let's build a product and then figure out how to sell it." Wrong! You are much better off considering how you intend to distribute a product before you build it. Before developing a product you want to verify your assumptions about your distribution channel.

Why? You will likely build the product slightly differently, depending on the distribution channel. It's tempting to keep distribution as an afterthought. After all, the product changes required to be compatible with distribution are often minor. However, just because the differences are minor from an engineering standpoint, it doesn't mean the revenue impact is minor.

When you build a product that is fundamentally incompatible with your distribution channel you can't sell it. A product is either compatible with the channel or it is not. It tends to be a black or white situation rather than "shades of grey."

Let's walk through some examples. Assume you run an enterprise software company. Your company is launching a new product to be sold to your installed base. To be compatible with this channel and target customer you need to provide robust migration and backwards compatibility tools. This will enable your existing customers to leverage their legacy data and applications. This would be 100% mandatory if the product is to be compatible with this channel. (And, with regard to creating "proof" of your promise, you'd probably want to have several documented case studies of successful migrations. In particular, you'd need to prove that the upgrade path is a low-risk activity. Otherwise, these customers won't buy—which is why figuring out the promise comes before product development.)

However, if you were selling the product primarily to new customers that don't own your legacy products you would take a different approach. In this case, there's no need to waste engineering resources creating migration and backwards compatibility capabilities.

Different distribution channels have different requirements, which impact how the product should be developed. It's important to know this in advance and not as a last minute, "Oh crap, they won't buy."

If you're an online company intending to sell your Web-based service online through affiliates or resellers then you have to look very carefully at your competitors' affiliate compensation plans. Online affiliates are just like money-hungry enterprise sales reps; they like cash—lots of it—and they want it right now.

So, if using affiliates is going to be your dominant channel, what kind of compensation plan do you need to offer? Do you need a big commission surge right at the initial sale? What do you do if your service is a monthly billing service? How do you reconcile the need to have affiliates get paid a lot right now, even though you only generate a modest amount received over many months? How do you solve this problem?

There are numerous options—some are product oriented, others marketing related, and the remainder a combination of the two. You could offer customers an immediate up-sell to a more expensive, deluxe version of your service. This increases the dollar value of the initial sale and gets more commission dollars into the hands of your affiliates. You could charge a "setup fee" that's paid in the first month—yet another way of increasing the first-month revenues to get some commission to your affiliates. The point is that you need to figure this out, or at least consider it, early in the process.

Distribution:
A Frequently Ignored Source of Additional Revenue

There's another reason why distribution is typically underestimated and overlooked as a major source of revenue growth.

High-tech and Internet companies are notorious for a "NIH" attitude (Not Invented Here). The underlying belief is that we can only sell products to our customers that we personally create.

But why?

Once you have an established, trusted relationship with a customer, you can sell all kinds of third-party products and services to them. There's no need to be restricted to only those products and services your engineering team can produce.

If you're concerned about brand reputation you can engage in white labeling and private labeling licensing opportunities. Or you can simply generate referral fees by introducing trusted third-party vendors to your account.

If you have even a modestly sized customer base, you can leverage your distribution channel by selling third-party products and services to your customer base.

Once again, the behind-the-scenes impact of selling more in-house and third-party products to existing customers is that you can afford to invest more to acquire new customers.

Now that we've gone over the basics of distribution, let's look at some common problems with distribution and how to solve them.

Distribution Problem #1:
How to Expand In-House Distribution

Solving distribution problems is easy to do conceptually, but implementing solutions is not always as easy. To expand your in-house distribution, whether it is via a field sales force, tele-sales, advertising, or Internet marketing, the principle is the same.

Work relentlessly to get your in-house distribution working on a small scale. Figure out what you did right. Standardize it and duplicate it.

The key to scaling up distribution is the concept I call a "repeatable unit." A repeatable unit can be a sales rep who's hitting her numbers out of the park, a marketing program that's working like crazy, or a tele-sales script that performs unusually well. The key with a repeatable unit is that you can, well, repeat it.

So if you have 10 salespeople and one is outselling the other nine combined, then you'd darn well better figure out what that one salesperson is doing to be effective that the others are not. Is that salesperson qualifying prospects in a different way than everyone else? What's driving the person's success? Is she more successful at getting more initial meetings with clients? If so, what's she doing that your other salespeople are not doing.

Or, does that salesperson get the same number of meetings, but converts those initial meetings into closed sales at a much higher closing rate? If so, what did she do differently? You have to figure out what that person did right. You've got to break it down step-by-step. Take apart each step of the process and examine each piece separately. Try to isolate what went right.

This is similar to an engineer troubleshooting or debugging some piece of technology. They systematically check each component until the problem is isolated and fixed.

I propose doing something similar, but instead of looking at this as a "trouble-shooting" exercise (find the source of the trouble and fix it), look at it as a "right-shooting" process (find out what went right so you can deliberately do more of it).

In a "right-shooting" process you systematically isolate and check each component of the process until you isolate the primary factor that went right. This is important because if you cannot isolate what went right you cannot duplicate it on a consistent basis.

You can use this exact same process for any type of distribution vehicle. If you have a great marketing campaign, do a "post-mortem" analysis and figure out what went right. Take the same campaign and cross-test it with a different mailing list. Take the same list and cross-test it with a different campaign. What drove the campaign's success? Was it the target audience you chose, the communication pieces, or a combination of the two?

If you got the audience right what's the specific demographic and psychographic profile of the people in that audience? Who are they? Where can you find more people exactly like them? Analytically isolate what works and duplicate it. That's the key to scaling up distribution.

Good Results Are Not Enough—You Must Have Good Results that Can Be Duplicated

There's a big difference between achieving extreme revenue growth temporarily and sustaining it for decades. In the former, all your team has to focus on is generating more revenues. But for an extreme revenue growth company, delivering strong revenue growth is simply not good enough. You must have revenue growth that can be duplicated on an on-going basis.

If you can't duplicate a good result it only means you got lucky. I don't mind having luck on my side, but I'd much rather have a proven, repeatable process. You must personally focus your team on this "duplication" aspect of revenue growth because they won't do it without your constant pestering.

You need to make this your mantra: "We don't need revenue growth; we need revenue growth that can be duplicated." That's the key to sustaining extreme revenue growth.

Turn Growth in Distribution into a Self-Financing Activity

The other key for sustaining extreme revenue growth is to make sure expanding distribution is a self-financing activity. Here's what I mean. Let's say you run a company that sells a business-to-business product. After extensive "right shooting" you've isolated and duplicated what's working well in your distribution channels. You have a "repeatable unit" in the form of a salesperson that follows your well-honed sales system.

Let's further assume that every time you hire a new sales rep that you pay $200,000 a year, the new hire consistently produces $2 million in sales each year for you. How many sales reps do you hire?

Of course, you hire as many as you can find that meet your criteria. This is an example of making expanding distribution a self-financing activity. Each time you replicate your "repeatable unit" of distribution it pays for itself, with money left over to fund the next repetition.

In this case, hiring one new salesperson generates enough revenue to pay for the next two salespeople. Those two, in turn, provide the cash flow to pay for the next four and so on. When you get the "micro-economics" of the repeatable unit to work on a small scale it makes scaling up distribution incredibly easy. This is another key for creating and sustaining extreme revenue growth.

This is also true for online businesses. Let's say you systematically "right shoot" your online sales process and have gotten your numbers to a pretty good level. Your numbers show that it costs you $1 in advertising to generate a single visitor to your Web site. On average, for every new visitor that comes to your site, your site generates $3 in revenues over the next 90 days. How much should you invest in marketing? As much as you possibly can, while maintaining the quality level of the prospects you attract and your performance metrics.

In both examples expanding distribution is completely self-financed. You take a well-honed, well-understood "repeatable unit" and multiply it. The greater the difference between the costs of putting an additional repeatable unit in place and the revenue it generates, the faster you can grow, completely financed from internal operations.

The repeatable unit is critical to scaling up. It's not enough to get your distribution channel to produce revenue; you must understand why it is working well so you can replicate it.

Incidentally, one of the reasons many fast-growing companies can't sustain growth is because they don't really know, analytically, what they're doing right.

You need to understand your sales and marketing process at a numerical level, the way someone running a

$1 billion dollar factory line knows precisely how each segment of the line is performing at any second of any day.

Distribution Problem #2:
Your Distribution Channel's "Repeatable Unit" Shows Only Modest Performance

So what happens if you're in a situation where the performance of your "repeatable unit" is mediocre? Your enterprise sales rep costs $200,000 but only produces $400,000. This is enough to put a little dent in your overhead but is not really a major contributor to your gross revenue. Or your online marketing campaign shows that it costs you $1.00 to get a visitor to your site, but you make only $1.20. It's a tiny profit hardly worth attempting to replicate on a wider scale.

In a situation like that you're better off not trying to replicate or scale up your distribution. In this case, your focus needs to be on two specific areas: trouble-shooting your sales and marketing process, and increasing your revenues per customer.

If your sales and marketing process is not performing well you have to continually adjust it until you can get the numbers up to a level that's worth replicating. Here's how to do it.

Break down your sales and marketing process into specific steps: Measure the performance of each step, systematically A/B test each step of the sales and marketing process, and look for the alternative that generates more sales.

I'll provide some examples in a second, but first let me define an A/B test. In an A/B test you alternate between two versions of a particular step in your sales and marketing process (e.g., Web site content, e-mail, direct mail piece, tele-sales script, etc.) and carefully track which one worked better.

This, frankly, is how 80% of all sales and marketing should be done. It should involve a systematic, analytical approach to continuously improving the results from your in-house distribution channel.

I've done extensive A/B testing (particularly online and in direct mail) in my own business and for clients. I have found it makes a significant impact on revenues and profits. In a typical on-going A/B testing effort I'll routinely increase sales 50 to 300%, when compared with the first version tested.

In one case that involved selling a product via the Internet it took ten months to get a version of the website to increase revenue per visitor by 500% when compared against the original version. The process involved testing nearly 50 different variations of the selling process. It was an excruciatingly detail-oriented effort that included testing prices, bundles, graphics, headlines, and even went so far as to test font faces and even the impact of indenting or not indenting paragraphs.

The A/B testing process is a "must do" for all selling and marketing that takes place in every distribution channel you use—online, print advertising, direct mail, telephone sales, and in-person sales. It's also appropriate for introductory meetings in business-to-business sales (but less so as complex deals progress and become more customized to the prospect's specific situation).

For example, if you do any kind of telephone sales in your company, everyone must use standardized telephone scripts—otherwise you're absolutely wasting money.

In fact, you shouldn't just be using one standardized phone script; you should always be using two at any given time—a "control" script (borrowed from the scientific community's use of "control groups" in double-blind experiments) that represents the best script you have to date, and a "challenger" script (akin to the "experimental group" in a scientific experiment).

This sounds like a pain to do, and it is, but it systematically and continuously increases revenues. The math is compelling, as evidenced in the following example.

The A/B Split-Testing Math:
How a 3% Weekly Improvement Generates
150% Annual Revenue Growth

One of the keys to creating and sustaining extreme revenue growth is to look for high return on investment opportunities in your business. These are opportunities that require only modest effort but increase revenues at a level substantially more than the effort required. Or, phrased differently, the key to extreme revenue growth is to look for the "little hinges that swing big doors." A/B testing is, without question, one of the highest-leveraging revenue growth opportunities you have in your business. The math is exceptionally compelling.

Here's an example: Let's say you run an A/B test every week in either a marketing campaign or in your sales process. On average, you find one version out performs another version by an average of only 3%. As far as A/B testing goes, this is a tiny level of improvement. It's common to get 15 to 20% improvement per attempt, particularly early on in the process.

You repeat the process again next week, and the week after, and so on. Some weeks you pick up a 6% improvement and other weeks you make no improvement. However, on average, you generate a 3% improvement each week in your sales and marketing process. If you keep this up for 52 weeks you'll realize a greater than 150% increase in sales per year—with little to no increase in marketing cost.

By getting only a modest 3% improvement each week through A/B testing you will continually double your revenues on your "repeatable unit" every 9 months or so. If you can pick up a 5% improvement each week you'll double revenues every 4 months. If you can get only a 1% improvement each week you'll post a 50% revenue increase, year after year.

All it takes is a lousy 1% improvement each week to post a 50% increase in sales, year after year. This is not about looking for major home runs, but rather being exceptionally disciplined about racking up tiny wins day in and day out. I can't emphasize enough that details matter.

Keep in mind that, in this example, the dramatic revenue gains do not include replicating your "repeatable unit." So, if you generate a 3% improvement in your sales process each week the "repeatable unit" will show a 150% increase in revenues at the end of the year.

If you keep the process up long enough your numbers will get to a point where the "repeatable unit" is indeed worth replicating.

At this point you can double your sales force or double your marketing effort every 12 months on a completely self-financed basis.

By combining a 150% increase in revenues for each "repeatable unit" with a 100% increase in the number of "repeatable units" you're posting a 250% annual growth, year after year. So, if you generate $10 million this year your run rate next year is $35 million.

Having gone through this A/B testing more times than I can remember, I can say it is fairly easy to find 10 to 30% improvements early in the process. However, over time it becomes harder and harder to find even a 5% improvement.

The point of this discussion is to illustrate that the key to improving the revenue productivity of the "repeatable unit" in your distribution channel is to continuously rack up a series of tiny wins. You do this by employing disciplined A/B testing as part of your operations.

Distribution Problem #3:
How to Expand Third-Party Distribution Partners

Show me the money. That's the most important thing to keep in mind when trying to scale up distribution through partners. Partners want to increase their revenues in a way that's consistent with their values and quality standards. The more you can match that, the more successful you'll be with partners.

In general there are two ways you can show them more money. First, they can profit by reselling your products (or by you paying them a referral fee or commission). Second, you can show your partner how every time a customer buys one of your company's products they automatically want to buy more of the partner's product or service.

The classic example is the partnership between hardware and software vendors. The more software you sell to a customer the more hardware they'll need. The more servers you sell the more data storage networks they sell. The more digital photo printers you sell the more photo paper they sell.

So, either way, you have to show partners a path to more money.

Let's start with paying partners directly through a value-added retailer (VAR), reseller, or affiliate relationship. Here's how reseller partners are paid:

$$(\$ \text{ Value of Sale}) \times (\text{Commission } \%) \times (\text{Closing } \%) = \text{Partner's Commission}$$

There are three ways to show these partners "the money":

1) Deliver a higher average transaction size than your competitors, and

2) Pay them a higher commission percentage,

3) Provide your partners with a well-honed sales and marketing process that converts prospects into buyers.

These are the three levers you have to play with in reseller partnerships. If you sell the most expensive offering in your industry, and offer the highest commission level (or wholesaler discount) and have the highest closing percentage in your industry, game over. You win. You will dominate third-party distribution in your industry.

So how exactly do you get to this enviable position? It all goes back to A/B testing. First, you A/B test your existing offering. You want to get the number of prospects that end up buying to be as high as possible. You then want to work on increasing your average transaction size. Look at selling via bundles, offering up-sell and cross-sell opportunities—all the while continuing the A/B split testing along the way.

You want to steadily improve the closing percentage and average transaction size. When you can lead the industry in both, it means more financial value is created when a prospect becomes one of your customers rather than a competitor's customer. When there's more value created there is more that can be shared, enabling you to offer a more attractive payout ratio to your resellers.

Even if you don't offer a higher payout percentage, your resellers will still be earning more through you because of the higher transaction size and higher closing percentage. It all comes back to the disciplined process of A/B testing.

When a reseller partner makes significantly more money partnering with you versus a competitor it becomes much easier to get more of them. Not only can you afford to invest more in partner acquisition, you will also find that a higher percentage of prospective partners become actual partners. This, of course, accelerates your revenue growth and increases revenues from third-party channels, which, in turn, provides you with even more resources to attract more partners. The process steadily cycles upward.

Distribution Problem #4:
How to Increase Revenues from the
Distribution You Already Have

The key to maximizing revenues and profits from an existing distribution channel is straightforward: Sell them more stuff. Sell them more of your products and services and sell them more of other people's stuff.

Your effective margins on sales to existing customers will always be substantially higher than sales to new customers. So, selling more to existing customers drives top-line sales and improves bottom-line profit margins, all at the same time.

This seems like such a mundane way to increase revenues. There's no magic bullet, no super-sexy partnership deal, no whiz-bang marketing campaign—just sell more to your existing customers.

In my advisory work with clients I routinely focus on this technique to generate an immediate surge in my client's revenues. For smaller clients with flat sales my track record so far has been an 81% success rate in doubling revenues within eight and a half months.

This result is achieved by extracting more out of the clients existing assets, rather than creating anything "new" (although getting the next doubling of sales is much more difficult). I mention this to impress upon you the idea that your customer base is almost always an under-utilized asset.

So here's the key principle to remember: When you have an established distribution channel and customer base, use them often!

Key Ideas:

- Distribution is one of the most under-valued and under-utilized methods for extreme revenue growth.

- Until you have access to a prospective customer, nothing else matters.

- To dominate new customer acquisition in your market, lead your industry in revenues per customer. The company that makes the most per customer is the company that can afford to spend the most to get a new one.

- To expand distribution focus on getting your distribution to work on a small scale (i.e., "the repeatable unit"), document what you did right, and multiply it.

- It's not enough to grow fast, you need to grow fast in a way that can be duplicated and multiplied. That's the difference between growth and sustained growth.

- Exceptional revenue growth comes from disciplined focus on using A/B testing to generate tiny incremental improvements weekly that add up to significant growth over time.

- To dominate 3rd party distribution, provide partners with a well honed sales process produced through A/B split testing, premium priced products, and a higher payout percentage—all of which puts more money into the distribution partner's pocket

CHAPTER 5

Create Easy-to-Sell Products
That Customers Love

Creating extreme revenue growth requires your
company to produce products and services that your
customers love and that are easy to sell through your
designated distribution channel.

Let's start with how to create products that customers
love. The key is creating products that fulfill the promises
made to the customer to generate the sale. In other words,
your product needs to actually solve the problem you
promised your customer you'd solve.

Sounds simple—and you'd think it is—but it's
shocking how often technology products do an
incomplete job of solving customers' problems. I've seen
numerous technological products (some with over five
years on the market) that never actually solve the
customer's problem completely.

As a "tech guy" it's downright embarrassing at times to
be associated with an industry that can't solve customer
problems.

Here's a simple story that illustrates my point: In my
family I'm known as a technology-savvy guy. I couldn't

stand it when, years ago, my mother would call me to figure out how to get rid of the darn blinking light on the VCR. You know the light I'm talking about. Anytime there's an electrical brown out (usually caused by a vacuum cleaner or hair dryer being used somewhere in the house), the VCR loses power for a second and the clock starts blinking 12:00…12:00…12:00. Yeah, that blinking light problem.

See what I mean? Everybody (and I do mean everybody) knows what I'm talking about, but no one ever fixes the darn problem. How hard would it be to guarantee that the darn clock will never blink again by adding a fifty-cent battery (that lasts 10 years) to the design so that you can make a promise people will notice?

Amazingly, even after companies have invested hundreds of millions of dollars in research and development they still can't fix a problem that impacts every VCR buyer.

As an industry we do a lousy job of solving 100% of the customers' problems. Sure, we have major technological breakthroughs, but invariably these breakthroughs solve 80% of the customers' problems. This leaves the customer to "tolerate" the remaining 20% of unresolved issues.

This chapter is not about how to build a product management and development organization—I'll probably have to save that for another book. It is, however, a chapter that describes the "big picture" principles that are absolutely essential for getting product management and development "right."

I'll also point out the most glaring product development errors made by technology companies and show you how to fix them.

The Cheng Rule of Product Development:
You Can't Build a Product to Solve a Problem
You Don't Understand

Let me illustrate this exceptionally powerful rule for effective product development with a story that I first read in 1995. I was so impressed with it that it has stuck with me all these years.

The story is about a guy named Kevin in the IT department of Wal-Mart. He had just turned 29 years old and was in charge of developing all the custom software applications for Wal-Mart.

The article I read, so many years ago, revealed how Kevin operated. During this time he was in charge of creating a wireless bar code scanning system. The system was designed to help the inventory clerks in the stores count inventory, without being tethered to a cash register or having to use paper and clipboard. In 1995 wireless systems like this were rare, so this was a cutting edge project. But that wasn't what caught my eye.

What caught my eye was Kevin Turner's product development process, which was impressive. He took his entire team of software engineers and made them all work as inventory clerks in the store for a full month before writing a single specification, requirement, or line of code.

Yeah, he turned super-star coders and developers into minimum wage inventory clerks for a month. These guys got up bright and early (just like their prospective end users did), went to a local store, got on their hands and knees with a pad of paper and pen, and started counting the number of boxes of Twinkies on the shelves that day.

Guess what they did the next day? You got it; they did the whole thing all over again—only that day they counted tube socks and t-shirts. The next day they counted bottles of Tide.

Despite decades in the high-tech world I have yet to meet an engineer who has literally "walked a month in the customers' shoes." Heck, I haven't met anyone who has walked even a day in the customers' shoes.

So, under Kevin direction the software development team responsible for creating a Radio Frequency ID (RFID) warehouse pallet tracking application would go out and drive forklifts for a month. The team working on the next revision of the point of sales/cashier system would work as cashiers for a month.

This would be deemed sacrilege in most high-tech companies. How many Stanford or MIT engineers do you know who would be willing to say, "Would you like paper or plastic?" for a month before writing any code?

When creating new products most engineers immediately begin by sketching technology architectures and high-level designs on a white board. The reaction they should have is to spend time living with the customer to make sure they really understand the problem before trying to solve it. Otherwise, your team will create a fantastic solution to a problem that customers don't actually have.

Yes, we live in a world of really cool technology and even cooler sounding buzz words. However, there is no technology in the world that can compensate for not understanding, in great detail, the problem the product should solve.

In Kevin's words: "On my IT team we are merchants first, technologists second." Even in 1995 I knew this was a guy who truly got it.

His high-tech product development process was, and continues to be, hands down the best process I've seen anywhere.

I find it terribly ironic that this approach comes from a company that isn't even a high-tech company. I suppose that's the point in the end—it's not about the technology, it's about solving problems. Perhaps we should re-label our industry from "high–tech" industry to "we solve customer problems—and happen to use technology to do it" industry.

As a side note, my gut reaction to Kevin Turner was spot on. Ten years later, in 2005, Steve Ballmer, CEO of Microsoft, hired Kevin Turner to be Chief Operating Officer for Microsoft. Kevin took over an organization with 38,000 employees and revenues of $50 billion a year.

There is a lesson here.

It's not about the technology; it's about solving the problem. And you can't do that unless you and your team really, really, understand the problem in great detail.

Simple Acid Tests:
How to Tell if Your Product Development Team Is Doing It Right

Here are some simple acid tests to determine if your product development team is doing things right. I've mentioned them elsewhere in the book, but it's important to include them here as well.

Ask your development team these questions:

- What's the first and last name of an actual person who typifies the target customer or prospect we're trying to satisfy with this release?

  (Hint: The wrong answer is no answer.)

- How many "person days" do you estimate will be required for this release?

- How many "person days" have we spent with actual customers and prospects making sure we understand the problems we're trying to solve with this release? Are you comfortable with this ratio?

On this last point, you'd be shocked at some of the ratios I've seen in some companies.

It is common to have 50 engineers working for five months on a release (that's 7,500 "person days" of labor), with less than five actual "person days" interacting with actual customers to really understand the problem the release is supposed to fix.

Product Development Tips

If all you do is keep in mind the "Cheng Rule of Product Development—You Can't Build a Product to Solve a Problem You Don't Understand," your company will have better product development processes than 90% of technology companies.

Every incremental hour, day, and week spent to really understand the customer and the customer's problems is exceptionally worthwhile.

A keen understanding of the customers and their problems will enable you to focus your engineering resources on solving the problems that matter most. This leads to greater customer satisfaction per unit of engineering resources utilized.

The following are other common product development problems and how to fix them.

Product Development Tip #1:
Features Should Be Aligned with
Specific Growth Engines

Product development's role is not to produce features; it's to enable revenue growth engines in a way that happens to involve building features.

It is better to deliver 100% of the requirements for one growth engine opportunity than to fulfill 50% of the requirements for two. While both approaches use the same engineering resources, the first approach has a higher revenue growth impact.

Many product development organizations have a list of all the features slated for each release. Instead of having a single feature list, the most revenue-focused approach is to create a feature list for each revenue growth engine.

For each product release, start by prioritizing the revenue growth engines first (not the features). The number one priority revenue growth engine should have all of its features included in the release, before any feature from the number two priority growth engine is included.

By shifting the focus from prioritizing features to prioritizing revenue growth opportunities first, you'll find that product development is much more aligned with driving revenue growth.

Product Development Tip #2:
The User Interface IS the Product and
Should Be Designed Before the Technology

When a customer pays for a product, the portion of the product they see—the user interface—is the product.

I can't tell you how many hardware and software products I see with terrible user interface designs. This happens because the "real engineers," with the super-high IQs, don't want to be bothered with the "soft" skills of user interface design; they'd rather work on the "really hard" engineering challenges. Usually, after the "hard work" is done, a user interface designer is brought in to make the powerful technology accessible to the end user.

This approach, of creating technology first and putting the task of enabling customers to use it in second place, is completely backward. All of the ideas in this book stem from the assumption that since the customer is the one with the money; we should start with what the customer wants first. Then we work backwards to figure out what we need to do to make that happen.

This "start with the customer first" approach also applies when it comes to product development. You start the process with what the customer wants to see and in the way the customer wants to see it. You create the user interface first, and then get the hard core engineers to create the "black box" that makes the user interface come to life.

The stuff that the customer sees and uses (interface, reports, API's) is the product. Customers could care less about what happens behind the scenes; they just want to know that if they give your system X information, the system will return Z outcome. (Surprise!)

This concept of "build first what the customer sees" is so simple, yet so many companies get it wrong.

I have a few theories on why the best practice approach isn't used often. You'll find three types of CEOs in most high-tech companies.

The first is a highly technical CEO who is highly familiar with the technology produced by his or her company. This type of CEO often has a natural tendency toward paying attention to what they know best—the technology. So the technical CEO will often instinctively think of the product first and the customer second. For this type of CEO, a process of "creating a technology first, then figuring out how to get customers to use it second" seems intuitive since it often mirrors his or her natural thought process.

The second type of CEO is the polar opposite—the non-technical CEO who doesn't know much about the technical side of things. This type of CEO will often rely on a strong VP of Engineering and defer technical decisions to that person. Because of this, the non-technical CEO may tolerate this approach because he or she may not have the background to feel comfortable over-ruling the VP of Engineering on this issue.

The third type of CEO is one who has an extensive background in both the technical and non-technical side of business (sales, marketing, and client service). This type of CEO is best suited for recognizing that the "technology first, customer second" approach is problematic and is technically savvy enough to address this issue with a technically oriented VP of Engineering. Unfortunately, this type of CEO is the rarest type, and, as a result, the "technology first, customer second" approach tends to pervade the high-tech industry.

However, it doesn't have to be that way. This book can be used as a guide and reminder for the technically oriented CEO to keep the big picture issues in the foreground. The book also gives tips for the non-technical CEO to help him or her manage a technology team without having to be a technologist.

Product Development for
the Non-Technical CEO

The act of managing a product development
organization is conceptually simple. Even though the
work done within a product development organization is
technical, the management of such an organization
doesn't need to be. Here's a simple primer on product
development for the non-technical CEO.

Every high-tech product has only two functions:

1) Accept information from the user (or from
   another system for middleware-type products),
   and

2) Produce an action or a report based on the user's
   request.

In other words, a product is like a mysterious "black
box." You put an "input" into one end of the black box
and the other end produces the "output" you expect. The
"stuff" in the middle (the "black box") is largely irrelevant
if the "inputs" and "outputs" are exactly what the
customer wants.

So, the key to managing a product development
organization as a CEO is to pay attention to the product's
"inputs" and "outputs." If both are exactly what the
customer wants, that's all you need to know as CEO. You
can delegate the "stuff in the middle" to your VP of
Engineering or CTO. This is not to say that the stuff in
the middle (such as compatibility, performance, and
scalability) isn't important—it is important—it's just that
from the CEO perspective, if you know the product does
what customers want it to, you can rely on your technical
team to make sure it's technically sound as well. I think

this defines the right level of involvement of a non-technical CEO in managing such an organization.

How to Tell If Your Product Development Team Is Doing It Right

In my career I've run product development, product management, product marketing, and corporate marketing organizations. I've also had the enormous advantage of being a technology buyer—so I've been on the receiving end of how most technology companies interact with customers. Through these diverse experiences I've seen many different product development organizations from many different perspectives. This has allowed me to see how a simple decision in product development ripples through to the sales and marketing organizations and, ultimately, to the customer.

In addition, my diverse experience gives me the ability to take a simple customer complaint and reverse engineer it to determine what decision, process, or procedure in the company created it.

As an example: Within the first seven minutes of a product demo I can often figure out a company's product development processes, biases, strengths, and flaws—often without even speaking to anyone from the product development organization. I can do this because bad (and good) product development processes are readily apparent in the product itself. Let me tell you what to look for to determine whether or not your company's (or your competitors') product development organization is doing the things that maximize revenue growth.

Start by looking at the user interface of your company's (or your competitors') products. Just by looking at the user interface you can tell an awful lot about a product development organization's collective beliefs, habits, and processes.

A customer-oriented product development team will create a user interface that's intuitive to the end user. It will accept the user's "inputs" in the exact order that feels natural to the end user. This is only possible if the product development organization creates the user interface first, and then builds the technical guts of the product to meet the requirements of the interface.

In contrast, a technology-oriented product development organization will design the user interface in the exact opposite way. The underlying technology will be created first and a user interface will be slapped on as an afterthought. Here's an example that illustrates this point:

The World's Worst Product Demo

Earlier in this book I shared my experience of evaluating and purchasing an enterprise accounting system for my employer at the time. When the sales team from one of the vendors came in to demo the product I asked the sales engineer to demonstrate how my assistant could use this very expensive accounting system to order me a $1 pencil.

When I made this request I expected to see the sales engineer log into the system as a user, click on a button called "purchase order," and click on "vendor name." I thought that, in the event the vendor did not exist in the system, a new vendor could be set up on the spot, and the buyer name and product to be purchased could be easily entered. Intuitively, I expected the whole experience to flow naturally in the order of how I, or my assistant, would normally handle a transaction.

Unfortunately, despite 23 minutes of trying, the sales engineer could not satisfy my simple request. Now, to his credit, he did tell me that the purchase order module was not preconfigured to demonstrate the feature ("Pencil," for example, was not in the system and could not be easily used in a demonstration).

My response was, "No problem—so let's see a demo showing how to add 'pencil' to the list of items that can appear in a purchase order."

He tried by clicking a bunch of buttons. Approximately 10 windows popped up, and then he announced he could not perform the demo because the user account (for my hypothetical assistant) was not set up for "administrative privileges," so the user wasn't allowed to add a new item to the list of items available for purchase.

I responded, "Well, geez that seems awfully cumbersome. But okay, I'll play ball with you. Show me the administration tools for changing the security settings so that my assistant can add 'pencil' to the system, so that the $1 pencil I want can be added to the purchase order."

Another 15 buttons were clicked and 15 windows popped up in the administration module (a total of about 32 on the screen at this point). After a total of 23 minutes the sales engineer finally gave up, embarrassed because he wasn't able to demonstrate how his product could handle such a simple request.

Here's a slightly technical interpretation of why the demo failed, and what it revealed about this company's product development philosophies and practices.

An ideal user interface should be process oriented. It should mimic the process the user intuitively wants to follow to accomplish a task.

This nightmare demo featured a user interface that mirrored the structure of the system's underlying database. The user data, product data, and purchase order data were all stored in separate database tables, and a user interface was created to match each table—completely ignoring how and when customers wanted to input particular pieces of information. This company missed the underlying idea that human beings don't think in terms of databases.

The company designed its user interface to reflect the underlying technical underpinnings of the system, rather than to reflect how real users actually work. The product development organization did not understand the problems of its customers, or they understood, but chose to ignore them. Either way, the results were not good.

I didn't end up buying the product because I was nagged by the idea that if the company totally misunderstood what its customers wanted there must be dozens of other flaws lurking somewhere in the system.

Was I willing to bet my career, and my reputation within the company, on this product? No way. Incidentally, even though this vendor was a very large company their sales for this particular product were extremely poor. After seeing the demo I knew why.

On a related note, if you go down to your corner software store and buy a $100 version of QuickBooks from Intuit you'll find an example of user interface that makes sense. Intuit's product development organization does a great job of understanding their customers' problems. As a result, their products actually solve customer problems—and sell well because of it.

I've met several people who've worked at Intuit over the years. From what I can tell as an outsider they have some very smart product development processes. They have usability labs where they watch products being used; they take notes on what buttons are clicked and in what order; and product testers are asked to say out loud what they're thinking. I'm under the impression that they also use eyeball-tracking studies to monitor how users' eyes move while using their products. (Where did the user intuitively look to perform the next task? Did they intuitively gravitate to the left or right?)

These guys really understand the customers' problems—much more so than most of the technology companies I see.

Product Development Tip #3:
The Most Important Feature in B2B Applications—
the ROI Report

The most important feature to include in software products sold to businesses is a report that shows the customer how smart they were to buy the product. It's a report that calculates, or estimates, how much revenue was generated or how much time or money was saved by using the product.

This is the one feature that proves the product is solving the problem for which it was designed. It doesn't matter if the product works as expected if the results aren't visible and obvious.

So, for anti-virus software products, the number one feature is the report that tells the user "five viruses detected and eliminated from your system." In effect, this tells the user they were so smart to buy your product; it just saved the customer from getting her computer wiped out!

Let's assume your product is a call center productivity application. You'd want to include an "estimated productivity improvement" calculator. This tool would enable the user to plug in labor and telecommunication costs, and compute cost savings based on reductions in, let's say, average call length.

There's another reason why you should include this type of feature in a product. In addition to proving to the customer that they made a good decision (and that you fulfilled your promise) this feature can also be used to better support the distribution of your product.

When you have a Return on Investment (ROI) calculator built into your product this feature makes for a killer demo. This actual tracking of return on investment gives the buyer a sense that, after they buy, they will know how much money they made or saved by using your product.

Technology buyers are always looking for "the visible win"—a project that is successful in a really obvious way. This is the path to career success as a technology buyer.

By the way, in case you haven't figured it out by now, the real promise you need to be making in business-to-business technology sales is "career success" or "career protection" for the final decision maker. This person wants to add one more item to the "win" column on their personal scorecard. Given the option of a highly successful project that's invisible to their boss or peers, or a successful project that's highly visible internally—IT buyers will always choose the latter. Always.

The ROI reporting feature gives buyers the ability to put together a "post project assessment" that proves their brilliance. If your product doesn't have that feature (or if the data is there but it's not easily accessible to the buyer), then you miss out on fulfilling a key customer desire.

This feature also helps in your sales and marketing process. It makes it much easier to get numerically quantifiable success stories from your customers, which provides proof that you can deliver on your promises. If you can show 93 detailed customer success stories along the lines of:

"We implemented your solution on March 2nd, 10:02 AM PST, and determined that exactly 60 days later we increased our call center productivity by 11%, enabling us to avoid over $1,172,013 in annualized salary expenses. Thanks a bunch. Your product really delivers!"

This type of numerically specific success story or testimonial is much better than the ones you typically see from tech companies: "You've helped us increase our call center productivity." "Your product is really, really great!"

No one believes testimonials that lack specificity. ROI reports and estimation calculators give you that specificity. It's a powerful, but underutilized, tool for maximizing revenue growth.

Product Development Tip #4:
The Second Most Important Feature
In Software Products

The second most important feature to have in your product is a highly visible, easy to access, "suggest a feature" button. This seems like such a simple and silly thing, but it makes a big difference.

Most software products do not have this feature and that's a big mistake. Most customers and users do not take the time to go out of their way to give you product suggestions. Product suggestions and/or improvement ideas occur to users when they're in the middle of using your product. They may be using a feature and they think to themselves, "Hey, this product really should do X."

The data collected from this feature becomes an asset and competitive advantage for your company. Think of it this way: With this feature in place the more users you have for your products the more insight you get into what your market wants and why they want it. It's one of the easiest ways to create and sustain greater revenue growth—and to make it increasingly difficult for companies in your industry to compete against you.

At the same time, if you have the largest user base in the industry but don't have this feature you are essentially underutilizing your user base asset. In fact, a smaller competitor with "suggest a feature" capability in their product will be much closer than you to hitting the bull's-eye in the market.

The effectiveness of your product development resources is multiplied when you have better information on the struggles and desires of your customers. This simple feature should be included whenever it's appropriate to do so.

Closing Thoughts

Use these product development guidelines and you will create products that are easier to sell and that your customers will really love. Don't forget that all of these tips stem from my golden rule of product development: "You Can't Build a Product to Solve a Problem You Don't Understand."

Key Ideas:

- The Cheng Rule of Product Development: You Can't Build a Product to Solve a Problem You Don't Understand

- Test the effectiveness of your product development team by asking to see a list of the customers they spoke to before they came up with the current product design

- It's better to complete 100% of the features needed to get one growth engine to take off than to complete 50% of the features for two growth engines

- The user interface IS the product and should be designed before the technology

- The most important feature in B2B applications is the return on investment report (aka. The report that proves the customer was so smart to buy your product)

- The second most important feature in software products is the "Suggest a Feature" feature

CHAPTER 6

The Sustainable Competitive Advantage

The fifth, and final, component of a growth engine is the sustainable competitive advantage. A sustainable competitive advantage is a "soft" or "hard" asset that's difficult for a competitor to duplicate. This enables you to extend the lifespan of a growth engine.

A soft asset might be a product development process capable of producing new product revisions in only four months, while the rest of the industry takes seven months. Another soft asset might be a method of recruiting and interviewing that consistently attracts exceptionally gifted employees. A hard asset could be a patent on a novel product design, a manufacturing facility, or a warehouse.

Here's an example of why creating a sustainable competitive advantage, while growing, is so important:

Sustainable Competitive Advantages Enable Sustained Revenue Growth

Early in the history of Amazon.com, CEO Jeff Bezos made a controversial move to build real brick and mortar warehouses all over the United States. At the time, the company was entirely virtual and relied on third-party wholesalers to drop-ship orders to customers on their behalf.

The decision was controversial because the company was young and not yet profitable. The addition of warehouses would not increase near-term revenues, but would make an already negative cash flow situation even worse.

I believe there were two reasons why Jeff Bezos made this controversial decision. First, it gave Amazon control over the "final step" of the customer experience—fulfillment—and gained numerous benefits for Amazon. To start with, Amazon would no longer be beholden to its primary wholesaler that fulfilled the majority of its orders. This move would also eventually allow Amazon to expand beyond just selling books. This fulfillment infrastructure would be a competitive advantage that could enable future growth engines that simply wouldn't be possible without it.

And second, without actually owning and controlling the fulfillment process Amazon was extremely vulnerable to competition. Any competitor could come along, put up a Web site, and sell books to be fulfilled by the same wholesaler used by Amazon—and many did. In other words, Amazon's competitive advantage at the time was slim, with serious issues regarding its sustainability.

So Bezos bet big on warehouses and caught enormous flack from Wall Street because of it. He simultaneously built six warehouses at a cost of over $300 million. That's a pretty gutsy move for an unprofitable company.

There was a reason for specifically choosing six warehouses and not three or ten. Six was the minimum number of warehouses needed to be within one or two shipping days of every zip code in America. He wanted to use his warehousing infrastructure to deliver a consistent, and fast, fulfillment experience for the customer. Six warehouses were what it would take to deliver on that promise. (Notice how Bezos had a particular customer promise in mind when contemplating this decision. As I stated earlier, figuring out the customer promise first makes all the subsequent decisions easier.)

Years later Amazon would enjoy enormous success using free shipping programs to acquire new customers and get existing customers to spend more.

On a personal note, I've noticed that, since I've taken advantage of these offers free shipping programs, my family's annual spending on Amazon has gone up steadily each year, at the expense of other online and local retailers. We started off buying only books from Amazon, but over the past few years we've purchased music, videos, computers, printers, cameras, gardening tools, toys, clothing, and medication. Amazon's free shipping program is so convenient that when I have to go to a local store to buy something I regularly ask myself, "Wait…can I get this on Amazon and have it delivered?"

That reaction is possible only because of Amazon's significant investment in warehouses and its fulfillment infrastructure. These competitive advantages have enabled Amazon to sustain growth for a much longer period of time than without it.

Today, Amazon's competitive advantages are more significant and sustainable than ever before. To compete with Amazon a competitor has to pony up $300 million just to match Amazon's fulfillment capability. This does not take into account all the other "hard" and "soft" assets Amazon has accumulated along the way, including patents, an enormous library of product reviews, digital scans of the first few pages of many of its books, an enviable affiliate network, and the list goes on.

The lesson of the sustainable competitive advantage is it's not enough to just seek a revenue growth engine that will produce revenues; you must also seek those opportunities that leverage your competitive advantages— making it harder for your competitors to copy you.

Here's another way to think about competitive advantages. Imagine you're competing in a car race across America from the West Coast to the East Coast. There are two ways to win:

1) Drive as fast as you can (akin to growing your revenues as fast as you can), or

2) Throw obstacles in the path of your competitors to slow them down (make it harder for your competitors to copy you).

When I imagine myself in this kind of race I can't help but see myself throwing buckets full of nails on the freeway behind me in the hopes of popping the tires of my competitors to slow them down.

Actually, the real image I have in mind is having my staff throw buckets of nails, kitchen sinks, and whatever else at my competitors while I have my engineering team build a pair of aircraft wings on the side of my sports car. While my competition is struggling with all the roadblocks I've thrown their way I'm building myself an airplane.

As I elevate competition to a whole new level my competitors are consuming their resources trying to deal with all of the obstacles they find in their path. By the time they catch up to me, assuming they do, my airplane has been built and I start to fly, and my staff continues to rain down debris to make their lives generally miserable. Yeah, I just love that kind of stuff and you should too.

Leverage a Competitive Advantage or Create One

There are two types of growth engines; small ones and big ones. A small growth engine might be a particular one-time-only promotion to your existing customers. It's a growth engine with a limited lifespan but one that's acknowledged and accepted. These "low hanging fruit" opportunities can boost a company's revenues with unusually low risk. However, the lifespan of these opportunities is often measured in weeks or months.

The second type of revenue growth engine is the big ones—cracking open new markets, going after a new customer segment, or solving a new class of problems for your existing customer base. The investment of time, money, and resources in the pursuit of these opportunities ranges from "significant" on the low end to "bet the company" on the high end.

For these types of revenue growth engine opportunities the role of the competitive advantage is important to consider. Each major growth engine should either take advantage of an existing competitive advantage or create one as a byproduct.

The reason for this is that the sustainability of your revenue growth engine is directly tied to your competitive advantages. If your pursuit of a revenue growth engine doesn't involve using or creating a competitive advantage, competitors can duplicate your efforts easily. This shortens the lifespan of the opportunity and makes it nearly impossible to sustain extreme revenue growth.

In contrast, when you leverage an existing competitive advantage as part of your growth engine it makes it difficult for a competitor to copy you.

Amazon.com provides a useful example: Several years ago Amazon.com introduced its Amazon Prime program. For a flat annual membership fee you could join the Prime program and receive free two day shipping on all of your purchases that came directly from Amazon (as opposed to its third-party retail partners).

This growth engine opportunity certainly had some risks associated with it. Amazon essentially made two key bets.

First, they bet that free shipping would cause customers to buy more things more often. Years of extensive A/B promotion testing demonstrated that this would happen, so the move was, in fact, not very risky.

The second bet was that membership fees and profits from these additional purchases would be higher than the actual hard costs of shipping everything via second day service.

So where does the competitive advantage come into play? Well, the Amazon Prime program took direct advantage of Amazon's six fulfillment warehouses that are strategically located within one or two shipping days of every zip code in America. Because of this competitive advantage the cost of shipping orders to Amazon Prime members is lower than the shipping costs most of its competitors face.

If I bought a book from any other online retailer with a single warehouse, and had it shipped second day air across the country, it would be pretty expensive. But when I buy a book from Amazon and request second day shipping, one of their warehouses is so close to my home that the actual shipping costs paid by Amazon is more modest.

In this case, the revenue growth engine (Amazon Prime) was deliberately and cleverly linked to assets (Amazon's six warehouses) that gave Amazon a competitive advantage. This relationship is important to recognize and appreciate.

A competing company could easily copy the promotional aspects of the Amazon Prime program by offering free shipping to its best customers. However, without the $300 million investment in six warehouses across the country, the competitor could not duplicate the underlying profitable economics of the program.

This is the key for creating extreme revenue growth that's sustainable over the long haul. You must either link revenue growth engines to exploit your existing competitive advantages or incorporate the creation of competitive advantages into your revenue growth plans. Either way, the sustainable competitive advantage is the key for long-term growth.

Key Ideas:

- How long you can sustain revenue growth is directly tied to your competitive advantages, and how difficult it is for a competitor to copy them. (The Amazon.com 6 fulfillment centers story)

- Every revenue growth engine opportunity should: exploit a pre-existing competitive advantage, create a new competitive advantage or enhance a pre-existing advantage, or both. This is the only sure way to sustain growth over the long term

Part II:
Managing Growth

CHAPTER 7

The 10 Times Test

The first challenge every CEO faces is, "How do I get this company to grow?" Once you solve this problem, the second challenge is, "Oh, geez. How do we keep up with all this growth?" Sure, it's a great problem to have, but make no mistake about it—it really is a problem that needs to be solved.

Scalable Systems

The key for managing rapid growth is to standardize your operations and design internal procedures that are scalable. Scalable operational procedures can handle significant increases in volume without re-design.

If you have a highly technical background you'll recognize that these terms come from the technical side of the software and hardware business. A scalable technology system is one that allows you to add many more users to your system without the system breaking under extreme usage.

A simple example would be an accounting software package, such as QuickBooks. The software is a fantastic system designed for up to a few concurrent users in a small business.

However, if you try to get 1,000 employees in a Fortune 500 company to use it concurrently it would break. It's not a scalable system (though it's a fantastic product for its intended audience and use).

On the Internet, a Web site that's scalable is one that can handle 100 users a day today, but 1,000,000 users a day next month, without a major re-writing of code or massive re-design of hardware architecture.

Scalable "People" Systems

This concept of a "scalable system" can also be applied to the non-technical aspects of a business as well. Every facet of your company—human resources, accounting, sales, marketing, customer service, consulting, product fulfillment, and technical support—is a system. I'm not talking about just the technology systems used in these areas; I'm also talking about all the manual work that gets done.

For example, when you integrate a new employee into your company you use a system. There are specific steps that need to be done—employee orientation, tax forms, employee benefit setup, e-mail address setup, provision of a desk, phone number assignment, and so on.

The key idea here is to recognize that literally everything in your business is, or should be, a system.

The "Bottleneck" Concept

An important concept to understand in dealing with systems is "the bottleneck." It's the part of the system that holds back every other part of the system. Executives who manage factories commonly use this term. When a portion of a manufacturing line is broken it creates a bottleneck that constrains the output of the entire factory.

For example, let's say you were running an automobile manufacturing facility capable of producing 1,000 cars a day. One day the painting section of the factory line has a problem—one of the two primary painting tools has failed, and only 500 cars can be painted a day, instead of 1,000. This is the bottleneck.

Bottlenecks can cripple any system. In our example, factory production drops from 1,000 cars per day to 500 cars per day because a single failure in the line.

It does not matter if the factory employs thousands of workers and every other part of the factory is running at full capacity; the entire output of the factory is constrained by this single bottleneck.

Another way to characterize the bottleneck is: A system can only produce at the capacity of its weakest link.

The "Bottleneck" Is Enemy Number One

The Bottleneck effect has important implications when it comes to creating and sustaining extreme revenue growth. It's impossible to sustain extreme revenue growth if you're not actively anticipating, looking for, and removing, the key bottlenecks in your company.

Let me give you some examples that illustrate this idea: Let's say your company has grown quite dramatically from $35 million in sales one year to $100 million the next. Clearly, your sales force was able to produce $100 million in sales. But can your consulting services and technical support departments handle $100 million in sales? If not, your customers will be disappointed in the experience. If the problem is severe enough, they will stop buying and your sales will automatically drop to a level your consulting and technical support staff can handle. The market has a tendency to automatically correct itself whenever you have a bottleneck in your customer-interaction systems.

Obviously, you don't want the market demand to be reduced to meet your company's ability to supply. You'd much rather increase your company's ability to supply to meet the hot market demand. Now, in a modestly growing company (say 15% per year), this is much less of an issue. It's much easier for modestly growing businesses to improve their systems and capacity incrementally. The challenge in a company with extreme revenue growth is the need for greater capacity—yesterday.

The Key to Scalable Systems: Remove the Bottleneck

The key to creating scalable operations is to continually look for, and anticipate, bottlenecks in your business operations, and to continually remove bottlenecks through process re-design, automation, or outsourcing. It's an on-going battle that you must deal with for as long as you intend to grow. In other words, you're always going to be dealing with this issue.

Remember, any time a system has a bottleneck it constrains the overall output of the system. So, if your capacity to recruit new employees is lower than your ability to generate revenues, you're going to hit a brick wall at some point. If your Web site can handle 10 million users a day—but your bandwidth agreements and data storage systems only allow 1 million users a day—the user who is number 1,000,001 is going to have a problem.

If your software development team has a habit of not documenting their code, this is not a big deal when the team consists of only five developers. But what happens when 300 developers have to work on the same code base? The inability of new developers to understand the work of their predecessors will create a bottleneck in their productivity. This will have a ripple effect across the company and will delay product releases. The final result is that revenue growth will be constrained by this bottleneck.

Here's the peculiar thing about bottlenecks: They're often hidden and difficult to detect. It's also common for underlying bottlenecks to be far removed from their more visible consequences. For example, if you had a slowdown in sales, would it ever occur to you that the reason is due to the lack of documentation in the source code of your product? So, what are you supposed to do? Go check the source code of your products yourself? Of course not.

Here's an easier approach. Train your executives and all your employees to be on the lookout for future bottlenecks and eliminate them before they can constrain growth. You will have to remind your team to do this constantly. It takes a little more effort up front to create a process, procedure, or system that scales well—but it makes such a big difference in the end.

The 10 Times Test

A simple way to get your entire team thinking about and removing future bottlenecks is to ask them a simple question: "If our business grew 10 times overnight, would you be able to handle it?"

Ask your VP of Customer Service: "If our new customer volume increased by tenfold, tomorrow morning at 9 a.m., would your department be able to handle it?"

Ask your fulfillment department: "If the number of orders needing fulfillment increased 10 times, could you handle it?"

Your VP of Sales should be thinking: "If lead generation increased tenfold by 9:00 tomorrow morning, could my team follow up on all of them?"

Don't be surprised if the first time you ask these questions you get a "You're crazy" look. In spite of the look it is the right question to ask. In fact, from a "managing growth" perspective, it is THE question to ask.

Here's why: It gets your team thinking about all the ripple effect issues that 10 times growth would cause.

We'll take a simple example: If your customer service department had to handle a 10 times growth in new customers each month, could they do it? If not, why? Let's look at the potential issues:

- We don't have enough customer service agents— we'd need at least 200 more.

- Of course, we'd need 200 new computers. But wait. Can we get 200 computers overnight? Even if we got them, can the IT staff set up 200 computers overnight?

- Wait. We need desks. Of course, people need desks…duhhh.

- Wait. We don't have the office space to house 200 new customer service agents. Could we get another building? Is that an option?

- What's the lead time required for getting more office space? It has to be 90 to 180 days to get good terms. Wait. Do we have anyone focused on just our real estate needs?

- This seems like a nightmare. Should we outsource our customer service to a third party that already manages 150 times more volume than we do? Or should we setup an "over flow" agreement with a 3rd party provider that automatically kicks in during our busy periods?

- But is customer service something we need to control directly, or is it a non-core activity?

- Would these customer service requests come in by e-mail or by phone? If by phone, our automated voice system was designed to handle only 50 concurrent calls—so the phone system would definitely fail.

- Oh yeah, if the requests came in by e-mail our e-mail case-tracking system would fail, too—we'd need to upgrade to the deluxe version of that system.

- Geez, how would we train these new agents? Right now we use a "buddy system" that pairs up a new agent with a veteran agent for a month. We can't have new agents training new agents, and we can't have each veteran agent mentor 10 new agents simultaneously. Should we move to a training course format? Would a self-directed eLearning training process scale better?

- How would we manage all these employees? We'd need a new layer of management, for sure. How would we staff it? What would be the ratio of "team leader" to customer service agent?

I always measure how good a question is by how many other questions it inspires. By this measure the "10 Times Test" is a really good question.

So ask yourself: "Could my company handle 10 times growth overnight?"

Almost every time I've asked this question I've gotten a frown in response. That's because virtually every CEO I know realizes the answer to the question is "No." Further, the question itself shines a bright light on all the potential bottlenecks.

It forces you to answer the questions about what parts of your business would "break" under a 10 times increase in business.

More importantly, you want your entire team thinking about what could be done today (with little to no incremental cost) that would make it easier to handle such growth.

The key to managing, and ultimately sustaining, extreme revenue growth is to anticipate future revenue growth bottlenecks and eliminate them before they actually constrain revenue growth.

Key Ideas:

- A system that is scalable is one that can handle enormous surges in volume or usage without falling apart. This term applies to people-powered systems as well as technology systems.

- The key to getting a system scalable is to remove bottlenecks that slow down the performance of a system

- Revenue generation is a system too—a system that is also constrained by bottlenecks

- Your entire company should be focused on anticipating, finding, and eliminating bottlenecks that constrain revenue growth

- The 10 Times Test: If your revenues increased by 10 times over night would your company be able to handle it or would your systems "break"?

CHAPTER 8

Standardize Your Operations

One of the keys to managing rapid revenue growth is through process standardization and scalability. Yes, this sounds like an incredibly detail-oriented and boring process. It is. BUT, if you don't do it you won't be able to serve your customers effectively under conditions of extreme revenue growth. The funny thing about pissed-off customers is they'll gladly fix your "we're growing too fast" problem by not spending any more money on your products or services. The purpose of this chapter is to show you the actual steps that will ensure this never happens to you.

What's a Process, and Why Should I Care?

A process is the mechanism for doing everyday tasks inside a company. There's a process for billing, customer complaints, order fulfillment, recruitment, and sales. Why should you care? Well, at the end of the day, your company consists of your people and your processes.

It's Impossible to Manage a Process
Unless You Standardize It

Process standardization involves documenting your processes and creating a single "best way" to do the most important activities in your company. In an engineering department you might have a standard process for naming software components and files. If you have 30 engineers, and every engineer does things his or her own way, you'll end up with 30 engineers who can't work together as a team.

If you have 70 customer service agents issuing refunds arbitrarily you're going to have some happy customers while others will be pissed off—and an accountant who'll be shocked at the lack of financial controls in your company.

There are two kinds of processes: Documented and undocumented. If you want to create and sustain extreme revenue growth you have absolutely no choice but to document your processes.

Here's why: If your processes are not documented and a key employee quits, your company is going to suffer much more than is necessary. This is what happens in "people-centered" companies and not in process- and role-centered companies.

When you document your processes and a key employee leaves, the knowledge of how to perform that person's role remains with the company. Sure, you lose out on the departing employee's ability to fulfill that role, but the knowledge of what the role actually entails day-to-day remains.

Process documentation can be fairly simple. It can be a one-page checklist of what needs to be done, and in what order, to reach the desired outcome. You can have a checklist or procedure for deciding when and how to issue customer refunds. You can have a one-page checklist for getting a new employee set up properly (e-mail account, keycard, business card, phone number, and so on). You can have a one-page description of key software coding and naming conventions. You can have a simple checklist of key factors to evaluate when performing an acquisition of another company.

For some this may seem like unnecessary paperwork and a hassle. All I can say is this tiny additional effort makes a big difference in the ability of your company to consistently deliver the results you want to deliver daily, regardless of what person is doing the work.

Basically, if the process is important enough to do well, it's important enough to document and to instill a little discipline in the process.

I think we can all learn from how airplane pilots operate. Even though a 747 pilot has logged 10,000 hours in her career she still uses a pre-flight checklist. Why? Because a documented, disciplined, repeatable process delivers consistently better results than trying to remember the right steps each and every time. If every major airline uses a standardized pre-flight checklist process when lives are truly at stake, you can certainly use the same principle when big revenue is at stake.

A Process That Stinks Is Better Than No Process at All

Process documentation has numerous advantages that become extremely relevant during phases of rapid growth. First, it allows you to instantly isolate the cause of any problems that pop up. If you have a customer who is unhappy with one of your customer service agents you only have to ask one question to determine what went wrong: Did the agent follow the documented process?

If the process was followed the cause of the problem is the process itself. However, if the agent ignored the documented process then the problem is due to the agent's inability to stick to the guidelines.

Documented processes make it easier to isolate the underlying causes of a problem and, more importantly, makes it much easier to fix.

Using the example of the unhappy customer, let's assume the customer service agent did his job and followed the documented process, and the customer still ended up unhappy.

In this situation you could make a one-time policy change decision and modify the documented process to eliminate future complaints of this type permanently. Insure that your staff follows the revised process and you'll never have to deal with that complaint again.

This ability to fix a problem once and for all is incredibly important in an extreme growth company. You simply will not have the time and energy to continually fix the same problems on a "one off" basis over and over again. Simple, quick, and long-lasting course corrections are only possible if your processes are documented.

When key decisions are institutionalized you do not have to continually re-invent the wheel for every new situation. Your company will automatically become more effective and efficient over time as each process gets honed and improved every single day.

Process Scalability

A process that's scalable can handle 10 times to 100 times more volume without falling apart. If you have a billing process that currently sends out 100 invoices a day, how easily could you send out 1,000 or 10,000 invoices a day? If your process can easily handle 10 times to 100 times the current volume without falling apart, then you have a process that scales well.

Documented policies and processes are much easier to multiply and scale up. For example, if you have your customer service processes, policies, and guidelines documented, it's much easier to grow from 10 to 100, or 100 to 1,000, customer service agents within a short period of time. At a minimum, all of your new agents will have a definitive set of guidelines that explain what they're expected to accomplish and how to do it. If your processes were not standardized and documented, trying to grow your customer service staff from 100 to 1,000 agents would be a miserable nightmare.

Just imagine 1,000 customer service agents all trying to learn your company policies through word of mouth. I get a headache just thinking about it—and I suspect you would too.

The key for making your processes scalable is documentation. Standardize your approach and then write it down. This will enable you to get new employees up to speed quickly.

The second part of creating process scalability is to initially design your processes to handle a much larger volume of business than you're currently dealing with. In every aspect of your business, simply ask yourself: "Will this process still work if the company were 10 times larger than it is today?"

This question is applicable to everything in your organization: from setting up new employees on their first day of work; how sales calls are made; and how you communicate with partners. Does the process still work at

10 times the current volume? Almost always, the answer you'll hear is "No." Don't be discouraged. It's a very tough standard to meet (which is the whole point), and the question is designed to force your team to think ahead.

When you know you can't handle 10 times growth overnight here's what you want to do next. Ask yourself and your team if you can make minor, low-cost improvements to your processes that would dramatically increase your capacity to handle more business. Or perhaps you should consider outsourcing an entire function to a third party who is better equipped to handle that function. Or perhaps some blend of the two would be the right choice.

Here's a technique borrowed from the world of manufacturing. Sometimes you can make a process scale better through "batching." Batching refers to the manufacturing process where, instead of producing something one at a time, you produce a whole batch at a time. Any time you buy canned soup, for example, that soup was not made one can at a time, but in a large batch and then divvied up into small cans.

Let's take the batching technique and apply it to, say, new employee orientation in a startup company. When you're a small company perhaps you put on your "head of human resources" hat and teach a new employee key values of your company that you want them to always remember. Each time you get a new employee you give a one-on-one new-hire orientation.

A simple batching technique is to set a standard time, say Friday mornings at 9:00 a.m., when all new employees get oriented at one time. The batching makes the process more scalable. Instead of conducting orientations one at a time you are able to orient 30, 50, or

100 people at a time. As CEO you may want to impart the key values of the company to new employees yourself, just as Bill Gates did for many years at Microsoft. This batching approach to new employee orientations has an almost unlimited capacity to orient and train new employees. It only requires the same fixed weekly investment of time, regardless of how many employees are oriented. That's a scalable process.

You want to strive for something similar in every aspect of your business—answering phones, administering health insurance, getting new customers up and running, processing customer complaints, billing, and the hundreds of other processes that occur in your company every single day.

What Makes "Professional Management" Professional?

Some of the clients I advise are first-time CEOs who founded the company they're running. Their companies became successful, and they suddenly found themselves in the unfamiliar role of CEO.

From time to time founding CEOs are asked by investors to step down and make room for a "professional manager" to take over.

So, what's the difference between "professional" management and its more entrepreneurial counterpart? While sometimes the outside CEO brings more raw talent to the table, often the primary contribution can be summarized in one word: Process.

The new CEO often knows "what to do" in certain situations that the founding CEO doesn't. This isn't a talent difference; it's just a difference in familiarity with important processes. The new CEO has a deeper library of best practice processes for getting certain things done and delivering the best results. This comes from the CEO borrowing the processes of other companies that the CEO ran or worked for.

For example, the new CEO takes a look at the billing process of the chaotic startup and realizes that nobody is tracking "days of aging" on account receivables. Even though the CEO isn't necessarily a finance expert she knows from her own mental library of processes that you must track these things to manage cash flow properly. Is such a CEO smarter than the founding CEO she replaced? Not necessarily. Does the new CEO have a greater knowledge and appreciation of key processes for a wider range of situations than the founding CEO? Often, yes.

Ironically, the timing of these "changes of the guard" at the CEO level is revealing. It often coincides happens precisely when the founding CEO has proven that a viable business exists. Investors try to inject an outside, process-oriented executive into the role of CEO just as extreme revenue growth takes off.

This further reinforces the point that the key for managing extreme revenue growth is through process standardization.

Key Ideas:

- Fast revenue growth cannot happen without scalable processes in place

- Having documented processes in places makes it easy to identify and fix root problems that constrain your revenue growth

- The difference between the entrepreneurial CEO and the "professional" CEO is knowledge of proven processes

CHAPTER 9

Every Problem Is A
Systems Problem

The key to managing extreme revenue growth is relying on documented, repeated, scalable systems. This brings up a specific skill that you, as CEO, must master. It's a skill that many CEOs do not have—mostly because it's possible to be successful in running a modestly growing business without it. However, it is impossible to manage an extreme revenue growth company without this skill. I call this skill the ability to recognize that "Every Problem Is Really Just a Symptom."

Revenue Growth Symptoms vs.
Revenue Growth Problems

In every system there are symptoms and problems. Typically, symptoms are highly visible while underlying problems are harder to see.

Allow me to illustrate with a simple example: A child is coughing and has a runny nose. The symptoms are the cough and runny nose. You can opt to treat the child's symptoms, but you don't actually solve the underlying problem. This means the problem could be likely to recur—again and again and again.

In this example the reason the child has a cough and runny nose is because she has a cold. That must be the underlying problem. Or is it? Why did the child get a cold? Is the cold the real problem or is there a problem underlying the cold?

If you investigate by following that child around all day you might realize that, at school, she hasn't been washing her hands before snack time. This results in her picking up germs from her classmates. It also explains why she's getting colds more often than her classmates who have better hygiene habits.

So, in this example, if you just treat the symptoms (the cough and runny nose) you've done absolutely nothing to solve the underlying problem—the hygiene habit. If you thought the cold was the problem you'd have missed the real, underlying problem.

This "symptoms vs. problems" thinking is critical in managing an extreme revenue growth company—particularly one that uses systems extensively. Here are some examples that show why this thinking is so important:

Example #1:
Two Bad Hires In a Row

Let's say the last two executives you hired had to be fired within six months. How do you interpret this situation? What's the real problem here? Was the problem the people that were hired? Or was the problem the system you used to select the bad hires? It's an interesting question, isn't it?

What if you find that you've made three or four bad hires in a row? Does your answer change?

Once again, is the problem the bad hire or is the problem the process you used to repeatedly pick bad hires?

Example #2:
Two Customers Complain
About a Product Defect

Two customers make the exact same complaint about a defect in your product. What's the problem? Is the problem the pissed-off customers or is the problem the product defect?

Is the problem the product defect or the process your company uses to detect product defects before customers see them? Is the problem the underlying product development process?

What's the real problem? It's important to continually ask and to continually look for the answer to the real problem. If you don't find and fix the "real" problem the symptoms are just going to come back, over and over again.

In this example if there's a flaw in the product development process it makes absolutely no sense to hire more customer service staff to handle the customer complaints, or to add more people to your quality assurance department to detect these problems. It does, however, make sense to isolate the originating problem and fix THAT problem, which will automatically fix all the downstream "problems" that are really just symptoms of the "real" problem.

Example #3:
Two "Super Star" Employees Quit

Let's say you have two amazing employees who quit on you suddenly. Is there a problem? Do you believe the reasons the employees gave you for leaving? Did both of these employees report to the same person? Is that executive doing something that drives away star talent but retains mediocre talent? Is the problem the departing employees or their boss? Or perhaps it's bigger than that. Maybe it's a company culture issue that inadvertently repels A-players but keeps B-players. What's the real problem?

Notice that how you define the "real" problem will dramatically change what you do in your attempt to fix it. It will also determine whether or not the "problem" occurs again.

Every Problem That Occurs Twice Is a Symptom

Here's the rule I suggest you follow: Any time something "bad" happens twice in your business assume the "bad thing" is a symptom of a bigger, more widespread, systemic problem.

As CEO you can't personally manage every aspect of your company. However, the great CEOs will manage at a high level but periodically take deep dives into the minutiae to flush out a problem. You don't have the time to do a deep dive on everything, so you have to pick and choose carefully. Anytime you see something "bad" happening twice in your business it's worth your taking a "deep dive" to explore it and resolve any systemic problems you uncover.

The Mother of All Problems

In a moment I'll share with you the most common problem of all. It's an underlying problem that appears in many forms. It's the underlying problem behind unhappy customers, poor sales, departing employees, and dozens of other highly visible symptoms. In many ways it genuinely is the mother of all problems. What is it?

It's the lack of documented, repeated systems for doing anything and everything in your company. Yes, I couldn't resist taking another shot at drilling this point home. It's all about your processes and systems.

If you have 50 customer service agents and each agent does things his or her own way you cannot consistently improve the performance of that department. If a customer complains there's nothing you can do to fix that problem on a permanent basis. Sure, you could replace the offending employee, but you have absolutely no guarantee that the replacement employee is not going to repeat the mistake.

Until you have documented and repeatable systems in place you simply cannot manage your company with the degree of control that's absolutely necessary in extreme revenue growth companies. Solve this "mother of all problems" and it makes everything else in your business infinitely easier.

Extreme Growth Magnifies All Problems

You must keep in mind that extreme revenue growth magnifies and multiplies problems. A problem that could be easily absorbed by a company growing 10% per year will blow up a company that's growing at 200% per year.

I like using the analogy of the Indy racecar driver. In the time an Indy racecar driver looks down at his speedometer and then looks up again, the 200 mph racecar has traveled the length of an entire football field. In other words, when you or I glance down at the speedometer, nothing bad happens. But if an Indy racecar driver does it at the wrong time it'll kill him. Just like the way extreme speed magnifies tiny problems in the cockpit of a racecar, extreme growth magnifies all operational problems.

The key for making sure small problems don't get out of hand is to remember that every problem that occurs twice is a symptom of a larger systemic problem.

Key Ideas:

- Every problem you think you have in your business is actually the symptom of an underlying systemic problem or flawed process

- Every "problem" that occurs twice is not really a problem at all; it's a symptom of a flawed process or system

- The mother of all problems is the lack of documented, repeatable processes that are continually improved and refined

- Extreme growth magnifies all problems and places great urgency on solving the little problems before they grow into big problems

Part III:
Sustaining Growth

CHAPTER 10

The Role of The CEO

The role of the CEO is to create, manage, and sustain revenue growth—preferably extreme revenue growth. In this chapter we will focus on sustaining growth, since it incorporates the other two. There are three key areas that require your attention:

1) Managing the portfolio of growth engines

2) Recruiting and assigning the right people to drive each growth engine

3) Keeping everyone accountable

In a nutshell, your job is to decide what needs to get done, who is going to do it, and to hold everyone accountable for getting the right things done on time. This is your role as CEO.

This role description is more "big picture" than what some CEOs are accustomed to, particularly founding CEOs. In startup companies it's common to have CEOs who get heavily involved in the details. The CEO may close deals, write certain pieces of code, and provide services to clients. In the earliest stages of growth this is necessary. However, it's important to recognize that spending 100% of your time "in the trenches" ultimately limits your growth because nobody else can pay attention to the three key "big picture" areas that you're responsible for.

At the end of the day, a proper balance must be struck. I definitely do not advocate delegating everything and not being involved; I think it's important for a CEO to periodically dive into the details because doing so enables the CEO to discover shifts in customer needs directly from customers.

You can always get others to sell, market, and create new products, but you can't get anyone else to manage your portfolio of growth opportunities, manage your talent pool, and keep everyone accountable. These three areas are your responsibility—and yours alone. This is true whether you're a three-person startup or a 1,000-person, publicly traded mid-market company. You simply can't delegate these areas to anyone else.

Role #1:
Managing the Portfolio of Growth Engines

As CEO it's your role to continually manage your portfolio of revenue growth engines. I should point out that for purposes of this discussion, growth engines include small, short-term, "quick hit" types of opportunities as well as major initiatives like entering new markets or introducing new products.

Some growth engines can be conceptualized, executed, and captured within 30 to 60 days. Others may involve a multi-year effort. The point here is that you have to actively manage this portfolio much like a mutual fund manager manages an investment portfolio. The key decisions that should be continually revisited are:

1) What projects should I approve and fund?

2) What projects should I stop because the ROI is no longer attractive?

3) In what order should projects be pursued, given resource constraints?

4) What are the dependencies between projects (Do I need the free cash flow produced by growth engine A to fund growth engine B?), and does this impact the other three types of decisions?

Role #2:
Recruiting, Allocating, and Managing Talent

One client of mine was looking at a legitimate opportunity to jump from $20 million a year to $100 million within 18 months. While the market opportunity existed, and he had many of the key assets in place, there was one major problem. Not enough talent on the team.

Here's what I said to him about talent and extreme growth companies: "Extreme revenue growth companies consume talent faster than a fire consumes gasoline."

If managing the growth engine portfolio is the equivalent of guiding the steering wheel of your racecar, talent is the high-octane fuel that makes the racecar go. In every fast-growing company I've ever been associated with talent was always in short supply. Always.

As CEO you must continually expand the talent on your team, wisely allocate the current talent to the highest potential opportunities, and manage your people to verify that they got the right things done. At the same time you must continually prune your team. This means getting rid of non-performers or people who aren't quite right for their role or for the organization.

Finally, you must also always keep your eye on the future. The people you hire in the early phases of the company may not be those who can take it to the next level. Managing people is a regular process that requires frequent attention.

Role #3:
Keeping Your Team Accountable for Results

The most boring and mundane task you will perform as CEO will be to hold people accountable for doing what they said they'd do, when they said they would do it. I say this is boring and mundane because, to most people, it's not nearly as sexy as inventing a killer business model or conceptualizing a breakthrough product. Enforcing accountability is the fundamental nuts and bolts work of the CEO; it must be done and it must be done consistently.

To keep things simple, think of it this way: Make the right decision about what needs to get done to grow revenues. Assign the right talent to each opportunity. If you do these two things then the only remaining obstacle comes from your people not following through on keeping their commitments.

How To Be An Effective CEO

These three areas are the "fundamentals" of being CEO. It's a fairly simple job to understand conceptually, but not always easy to live, breath, and practice day in and day out.

Let's dig into each of these areas in greater detail in the next few chapters.

Key Ideas:

There are three roles for the CEO that can not, and should not, be delegated to others

- **Role #1:** Managing the portfolio of growth engines

- **Role #2:** Recruiting, allocating, and managing Talent

- **Role #3:** Keeping your team accountable for results

CHAPTER 11

Managing The Growth Portfolio

One of your key roles as CEO is to continually manage the portfolio of growth engines in your company. At first glance this does not seem like a particularly time-consuming task. In fact, it should be one of three all-consuming tasks you focus on. The other two are managing your people and keeping your team accountable for results.

Here's why many CEOs severely underestimate the scope and complexity of managing their growth portfolio. Many CEOs think, "I have three products. That's three growth engines, right?" Not quite. Keep in mind that a growth engine consists of five components:

1) A target customer

2) A promise

3) A distribution channel

4) A product or service

5) A sustainable competitive advantage

If you only equate a growth engine to a product you're missing out on 80% of your revenue growth opportunities. This is a big deal.

You can take an existing product and push it through a new distribution channel—that is a growth engine.

You can take an existing product and existing distribution channel and simply find your existing target customer a new way to use your product (like buying aspirin for heart disease prevention and not just as a headache remedy). Slap a legitimate new promise on an old product and you've got a growth engine.

You can segment your target customers into segments that are more tightly focused than your competitor's approach. While keeping the product the same (or making only superficial changes) you could target your promise to that segment much more precisely than competitor's more generic promise could. Do this and you've got a new growth engine—in fact, several new ones.

If your company is an online digital video disc (DVD) subscription rental business, like NetFlix, this would be the equivalent of NetFlix for Kids, NetFlix for Parents, NetFlix for Women, NetFlix for Christians, or NetFlix for Romantics.

You can change the first four elements to create an entirely new growth engine. Apple did this in their joint venture with Nike to create an iPod for walkers and runners. It's the same core iPod with an add-on module that tracks how far and how fast you walk or run. This only works with special iPod-compatible Nike running shoes (which, incidentally, cost 70% more than the regular ones).

The entire kit—iPod, add-on module, and special shoes—is sold through shoe stores! (I'll bet you didn't think of that distribution channel, did you? I know I didn't.) Presto, you've got a new growth engine.

Actually, the iPod for runners got my mother to buy an iPod and her iPod is cooler looking than the one I got! How the heck did that happen? Somebody, somewhere, obviously did something clever to pull that one off.

This is the stuff that happens when you manage your revenue growth engine portfolio. You simply mix and match the five components of a growth engine and "invent" new growth engines.

Inventing a new growth engine is always an exercise in being clever and strategic—and not always an exercise in research and development. It's an important distinction to keep in mind.

You can invent new growth engines if you sell hardware, software, or services. It works as well when selling to consumers as it does selling to other businesses.

If you sell hardware-based Internet security devices you could create a growth engine around personal firewalls or a small home/office firewall. Who cares if the physical device is the same as your entry-level enterprise firewalls? You could create a growth engine by taking the same physical device and selling it to physicians' offices as a way to be "HIPPA compliant" (HIPPA is a series of laws requiring physicians to safeguard the privacy of patient data). It does protect patient data, doesn't it?

You could build an entire distribution channel to target medical practices without changing the product (though the marketer in me would be tempted to slap a "HIPPA Compliant Firewall" sticker on the device).

Hopefully, you can see that the possibilities for growth are truly endless—which is precisely why managing your portfolio requires so much of your attention.

Personally, I think the whole attitude of growth being constrained by "engineering" is a bunch of crap. Revenue constraints come from a lack of awareness of the components of a growth engine that don't require engineering resources.

The problem is very few people in high-tech and Internet companies think this way. It's an exceptionally product/engineering-focused culture that ultimately leaves a lot of uncollected revenue on the table.

Just because everyone else thinks this way doesn't mean you have to. Heck, if my mom has an iPod that's cooler than mine then someone was doing something right when it comes to revenue growth.

The Four Portfolio Management Decisions

When managing your portfolio of growth opportunities there are only four basic decisions you need to make:

1) Add a growth engine to your portfolio

2) Remove an underperforming growth engine from the portfolio

3) Modify the scope, expectations, or resources of an approved growth engine

4) Change the scheduling or sequencing of how your growth engines are pursued

The portfolio should be managed and revisited on a regular basis. I generally like doing it on a monthly basis. However, the frequency will depend on the growth rate of your company, the size of your company, and the seniority level of the leaders of each growth engine.

If you're running a Fortune 500 company and each of your key executives is running a $1 billion business then a quarterly "deep dive" review is often reasonable— particularly if each of your key executives has the skills to run their own Fortune 500 company.

If you're a five-person startup that's growing like crazy, then a month is an eternity. A check-in twice a month, or, in some cases, every week, might make sense, especially if there's a high likelihood that new information could surface in that time frame that would cause you to re-prioritize your growth opportunities.

Decision #1:
Adding a Growth Engine
to Your Portfolio

The decision to add a growth engine to your portfolio should not be made lightly. This is not a situation where more is better; it's about effectively achieving your revenue objectives with the simplest, lowest risk approach possible.

There are many factors that need to be considered for each prospective growth engine. Some criteria need to be considered on an absolute basis, such as determining if the project is a good fit with your company's area of expertise.

In other situations, such as evaluating multiple opportunities, you have to consider things like which opportunity has the most attractive risk/reward ratio.

Let me start by listing the types of factors you'll want to consider. I'll then elaborate on the criteria that many CEOs either miss or significantly underestimate, which causes them to make bad decisions.

What Makes a Good Growth Engine?

- Attractive revenue potential relative to the financial resources required

- Attractive revenue potential relative to the people required

- Growth engine has been validated with market testing and feedback (we know this will work in the real world)

- Fills a "gap" in the marketplace, so we can offer a unique promise to target customers

- Opportunity is within the company's capabilities

- Leverages a pre-existing competitive advantage

- Creates, enhances, or strengthens a competitive advantage

How to Choose Growth Engine Opportunities for Your Portfolio

Just because an attractive growth engine opportunity exists it doesn't mean you should fund it. You must take into consideration the investments made in, and risks taken for, the opportunities already in your portfolio. Here are some additional considerations:

- Do we have the financial resources and people to fund this opportunity? Can we make available the financial resources and people to fund this opportunity?

- How much risk is involved in this single opportunity? With the addition of this opportunity how much risk do we have in the portfolio overall? If this opportunity fails, can we absorb the loss, or are we essentially "betting the farm" on this one?

- How much management attention and focus will be required? Does the revenue potential from this growth engine justify the dilution of focus on our existing growth engines?

Distraction Is the Enemy of Focus

Many CEOs underestimate the importance of focus and of avoiding its evil sidekick, "distraction." Exceptional focus is one of the keys to creating and sustaining extreme revenue growth.

There are only so many things you and your team can pay attention to at one time. Most projects end up being more difficult, complicated, and time-consuming than initially assumed. I've never heard of any technology company shipping a product release early. Have you?

Of course, not all revenue growth engines rely on engineering. But even for opportunities that rely more on marketing and distribution you still need "A" players on your team to focus on delivering the results you want.

It's also important to recognize the difference between staffing a project with people and assigning an "A" player to focus on delivering results. The former is about getting activities done; the latter is about getting "results" done.

As you'll see in the next chapter on people this is the reason why fast-growing companies consume talent like a fire consumes gasoline. "A" players are always in short supply. Always. Even when you recruit like crazy "A" players will be in short supply. So, you need to be careful about any growth engine opportunity that dilutes the focus your "A" players have on existing opportunities.

Decision #2:
When to Remove a Growth Engine From Your Portfolio

Killing growth engine opportunities that aren't working is a necessary part of the portfolio management process. Most CEOs will eagerly approve chasing a new opportunity but will be slow and reluctant to kill one.

What they don't appreciate is you can't assign your top talent to a new opportunity without killing the stagnating projects they're currently assigned to.

In general, it is easy to kill growth engine opportunities that fail miserably. The much harder effort is to kill growth engines that show a little success or growth engines that used to succeed wildly but now perform more modestly.

A Minimum Return on Investment

Over a decade ago I was a consultant at McKinsey & Company where I advised executives that ran divisions of Fortune 500 companies. Typically, these executives had businesses generating $100 million to $500 million in revenues.

There is one practice I found to be very common in Fortune 500 companies that does not appear nearly as often in smaller, fast-growing companies. This practice involves using a minimum "return on investment" standard that must be met for each growth engine to be funded (or to continue to be funded).

Each client I worked with used a slightly different metric, but they all used the same principle—you need some type of minimum return on investment criteria for what kind of opportunity you'll fund. In venture capital firms they use the "Internal Rate of Return." In capital-intensive industries, like manufacturing, you'll often see "Return on Assets" being used. In service-oriented companies you'll see variations of "Return on Equity" or "Return on Invested Capital."

There's an important reason for having a minimum return on investment threshold.

The most obvious reason is to know which growth engine opportunities to approve and add to your portfolio. The slightly less obvious reason is to know when to kill a project to free up resources that can be dedicated to other opportunities.

A struggling growth engine should not be killed the moment its performance falls below the minimum threshold. However, such a project should be examined rigorously to determine why it has failed to meet expectations. Is there new information about the market? Do you have the wrong person leading the effort?

The threshold exists as a way to trigger a "yellow flag" and to force a critical examination of the project in progress. If the situation is unlikely to improve enough within an acceptable time frame then look to kill the project and deploy the resources elsewhere.

Just like a gardener that continually prunes his garden to get it to thrive, you must do the same to your revenue growth portfolio.

Decision #3:
Making Midcourse Corrections to Growth Engines

Making adjustments to growth engines already in your portfolio is the third type of decision you'll face. Generally, such an adjustment is made after a project has been launched and new information becomes available for consideration. Sometimes the data involves new market feedback about an opportunity. Other times real world testing of assumptions yields new information that needs to be considered. When such a re-evaluation takes place you typically have three options:

1) Revise the expectations you have for the size and timing of the revenue impact of the growth engine

2) Revise the level of resources you plan to invest in the project

3) Revise the approach to capture the opportunity

These decisions should always be considered any time a revenue growth engine opportunity falls beneath its minimum return on investment threshold. In addition, these decisions should be considered for all the opportunities in your portfolio (even the ones succeeding), at least once or twice a year, as standard procedure.

One of the reasons you want to critically analyze projects that are going well is that you may realize that you're under-investing in those projects. It might make sense to dramatically increase your investments in those projects, which, in turn, may necessitate scaling back on other projects not performing as well.

Decision #4:
Re-sequencing a Series of Growth Engine Projects

As your company gets larger you'll have a more complicated portfolio to manage. Often you will need to take cash flow produced from a mature growth engine to fund the cash requirements of an earlier-stage growth engine.

This can be a complicated series of sequencing moves, much like stringing together a series of elegant maneuvers on a chessboard. This assumes, of course, that all projects will go smoothly. When some fail (and invariably some do) you will have to re-prioritize your opportunities and re-sequence the order of your plan.

For example, if you've decided to expand internationally and intend to use the profits from France to fund expansion in Italy you may have to revisit that decision if the France numbers come in lower than expected.

In fact, when a major growth engine's numbers come in lower than expected you certainly have to re-consider all the projects whose funding was to be provided by this now-struggling growth engine.

In general, the more linkages you have between growth engine opportunities the more likely you'll need to re-visit the sequencing issues as problems pop up.

Closing Thoughts

As you can see, managing your portfolio of growth engines is mentally taxing and critical work. It's the kind of work that only you can do (with input from your staff). It's not something that you can delegate entirely to someone else. If you don't pay attention to it, nobody else will.

There is one more thing you'll notice about managing growth engine opportunities. The key constraint is often not having enough talent on board capable of delivering results.

There's a big difference between getting "things" done and getting "revenue" done. One involves being busy, while the other involves being effective. The two are not the same.

One of the keys to sustaining extreme revenue growth is managing your team's talent. You need to find it, recruit it, manage it, and keep it. If you can't do that you can't win. Period. Let's look to the next chapter for details on recruiting and managing talent.

Key Ideas:

- Managing your portfolio of revenue growth engine opportunities is an active, highly time consuming process, and most CEOs don't devote enough time to it.

- A new growth engine opportunity can be created by modifying any of its 5 key components: the target customer, the customer promise, the distribution channel, the product, and the competitive advantage

- Most high-tech and Internet companies mistakenly over-focus on the importance of the product at the expense of the other components of a growth engine

- The key to managing a growth engine portfolio is not to have as many growth engines as possible, but to effectively deliver on your growth objectives with the simplest possible portfolio

- A key to knowing when to remove a failing or mediocre performing revenue growth engine is to establish a minimum return on investment requirement for your entire portfolio

CHAPTER 12

Talent:
The Rocket Fuel For
Sustained Growth

Fast-growing companies need a lot of talent to grow and to sustain that growth. I'll kick off this chapter with specific processes I recommend for hiring your executive team. Then I'll shift to how hiring and managing people at all levels of the company should be done.

The Four Keys To Staffing the Executive Team

- **Key #1:** Know yourself before you start assembling your executive team. This may seem an odd place to start, but it's an important part of the process. You need to have an accurate assessment of your own strengths, weaknesses, and biases.

- **Key #2:** Plan to spend your time day-to-day using your exceptional talents, and staff a team around you who will cover your weaknesses, including those things you're competent at but don't perform exceptionally well.

- **Key #3:** Keep in mind that when you're staffing your executive team you are not hiring executives who will stand alone—you're hiring people who will work as part of a team. This means not isolating your evaluation of a prospective hire but basing your evaluation in part on who is already on the team—a very important distinction.

- **Key #4:** Hire people for their strengths and be willing to tolerate their weaknesses, particularly if other members of the team can offset their weaknesses.

Here's why using these four keys to staffing your executive team makes a difference: In highly competitive markets, all else being equal, average talent gets you average results, while exceptional talent gets you exceptional results.

Here's the odd thing about people with exceptional talents—they often come with great weaknesses. If you simply avoid the people with weaknesses you end up missing out on hiring exceptional talent.

The key to getting the most revenue growth out of a pool of talent is to put people in roles that leverage their exceptional talents; this means matching people with their highest producing activity.

Don't worry too much about their weaknesses—especially if their weaknesses do not impact the results they deliver while in the role you've assigned them to. Each member of your executive team should have his or her weaknesses offset by other team members' strengths—and vice versa.

For example, if your VP of Sales knows how to "hunt the big deals" but is somewhat weak on the administrative side of sales forecasting, it doesn't mean you shouldn't hire her. You could have a Chief Financial Officer (CFO), or perhaps a Director of Sales Operations, who is very good at sales forecasts and have the two work together.

Inside Talent vs. Outside Talent

You will want to have talent in-house, as employees, whenever the nature of the work is predictable, consistent, and repetitive. You want to leverage outside advisors, vendors, and contractors for work that tends to be:

1) One-time in nature, or

2) Requires expertise not in your company's "core" area of expertise.

Everyone in your company should be spending their time using his or her exceptional skills and delegating the rest, just as you should.

Know what your company is good at and stick to it. Outsource the rest of the work (things your company is not good at or is merely competent in performing) to those who are exceptional at doing that kind of work. This way, you maximize your valuable resources by having your team focus exclusively on what your company does best.

A-players vs. B-players

Fast-growing companies require A-players, and lots of them. So what exactly is an A-player, and how is that person different from a B-player? A B-player does what he or she is told, does it well, and does it on time. If something unexpected happens, however, the B-player comes back and asks, "What do you want me to do now?" In contrast, an A-player solves any unexpected problems that pop up in the course of achieving the results you desire and tells you about it after the fact. Or if an A-player comes to you with a problem, she'll come with a recommended solution too.

In other words B-players focus on getting activities done, A-players focus on getting results done. I've always said that one A-player is worth five B-players.

I once heard something attributed to Steve Jobs—a comment that I haven't been able to verify. It goes, "Whoever said one A-player is worth five B-players is dead wrong. One A-player is worth 50 B-players!"

Several Characteristics of A-players and B-players

- A-players like working with other A-players.

- A-players like hiring other A-players because it means there's less work for them to do.

- A-players are motivated by exciting work, a peer group of other A-players, and an opportunity to grow their skills.

- A-players value winning more than ego, power, and politics.

- A-players' salaries are only slightly higher (10 to 40% is common) than B-players, but deliver 300 to 500% greater results.

- B-players do not like hiring A-players for fear of being shown up.

- B-players like hiring C-players so they feel smart in comparison (and C-players like hiring D-players for the same reason).

A-player Roles vs. B-player Roles

Here's an interesting question: Should you aim for a company full of A-players, or is having some B-players acceptable, even preferable?

As a general rule, the answer depends on the kind of growth rate your company intends to pursue. If you are in an industry that's not growing, and the company itself is not growing, having A-players in key positions and B-players in labor-repetitive roles can make sense.

In fast-growing technology fields you're always going to have a shortage of talent. Seeking to have A-players in all functions of your business makes sense. Let's take the role of customer service agent.

In a mature company, a B-player is going to be fine for that role. In a fast-growing company, there are going to be all kinds of department projects, cross-functional projects, and numerous growth engine opportunities that have a customer service component. Having A-players in customer service who can be peeled off for special projects is essential. Further, as the company grows, the department itself will grow, which means there will be a need for team leaders, shift leaders (for 24/7 operations), and numerous other leadership roles that will be required for growth. Having a pipeline of A-players will be an asset.

You can argue that you can always go for an outside hire when you need an A-player. That's true. However, in an extreme revenue growth company you need to do both: promote A-players from within and hire them from outside the company. As I said, you simply can't have enough A-players.

Fire the Bottom 10% Every Year

The process of hiring talent is an imperfect one, and, invariably, bad hires linger longer than they should. While bad hires, or even just "so-so" hires, should be let go immediately, often so many things are going on that the firing gets delayed.

Here's a process for managing top talent that I happen to like a lot. It's a bit controversial and I personally don't understand why. The practice is to fire the bottom 10% of your staff once a year.

I first discovered this practice when I worked at McKinsey—a company known for its ability to recruit and retain exceptionally talented people.

For example, the interview process I went through to get into McKinsey was pretty intense—a total of 13 interviews. Out of 400 people who applied from Stanford University, they rejected 396 of them. They believed in hiring the "best of the best" and their selectivity numbers certainly backed up their claim.

What was most interesting about McKinsey was what they did with the "best of the best" after they hired them. Every two years the firm fired the bottom 25% of the consulting staff, at every level of the firm (roughly 13% each year). To most outside observers this seemed pretty harsh, but it had several good consequences that were not always obvious, or appreciated.

Every two years there were suddenly a lot of vacant roles that needed to be filled. This allow high-performing, up-and-coming super stars to move up and kept the most talented people interested in staying with the firm. If the bottom 25% weren't fired then there would be no room for promoting the up-and-coming stars and the best people would become frustrated by the lack of opportunity and leave to work elsewhere. This process focused people on performing at their best and delivering results.

To some this apparently harsh process seems like some version of "survival of the fittest." There's no question it was, but my response has always been: "In your industry, my guess is that only the strong survive." It's just marketplace reality. If you don't manage your people in a way that reflects marketplace reality, and your competitors do, you're at a major disadvantage.

Since working at McKinsey was my first job out of college, I simply assumed all companies managed their people this way. I later discovered that this was far from the truth.

Here's why I like the tough people-management process at McKinsey: First, I like the process because it's a "process." It's a specific activity, on a specific schedule, to achieve a specific result. And second, I believe retaining "so-so" hires is like keeping clothing that no longer fits you or isn't in style; it just accumulates in the back of the closet, taking up space. You then have to periodically "spring-clean" to free up room for new stuff (or to free up the budget to hire new people—preferably A-players).

Hire Slow, Fire Fast

As a philosophical rule you want to be very careful when hiring; it's a critical decision, and you want to guard against the temptation to get a "warm body" into the role because you're growing so fast. If you fall for the temptation of putting mediocre people in key roles your "growing too fast" problem will solve itself. That's because B-players will under-perform and slow down that growth for you.

How to Hire Right

Hiring right a key skill that you need to master. I'm going to describe a five step hiring processes that I personally use and recommend to my clients.

Hiring Step #1:
Define Results You Want From a Role
Before Recruiting For It.

The number one reason for making bad hires is that companies do not have a clear understanding of what they expect from the role. Most companies write "job descriptions." I insist that all my clients write "results descriptions." After all, you're not looking to hire someone for a "job"—you're hiring someone to produce results.

If you're not clear on the result you want then don't complain if your new hire doesn't achieve it.

A job description tends to focus on specifics, like "years of experience" or "must have X degree." I look at those job descriptions and I just laugh: Who cares about all that stuff?

I usually cross out all the "human resource" language and write the words, "Must produce these results," and I tack on a list of all the results that person must produce within six months or they're fired. (I don't literally do it, but it's what I'm thinking.)

Every time I've used this type of results description (in lieu of the traditional job description), I'm surprised by the compliments I get from the candidates themselves—especially the A-player candidates.

They're surprised at the precision and clarity of what will be expected of them. Often, in the interview process they will point to specific experiences of theirs that demonstrate they can accomplish every desired outcome listed.

The "result description" excites A-players because it conveys to them the idea that the hiring company has their act together. It leads them to think, "If a company is this on top of things in the recruiting process, it must be filled with other A-players." This is especially appealing to A-players.

The other reason this recruiting process appeals to A-players is that there's a sense of objectivity about it. It makes it clear to the A-player that, to succeed, he or she will need to accomplish X.

There is no brown-nosing, kissing up, or politics needed to get ahead; you just get these seven things done within six months and you'll be a hero.

They love that stuff.

Hiring Step #2:
Identify the Key Skills and Knowledge Needed to Produce Each Result

Once you have a written "results description" written you want to systematically analyze each particular outcome you want, and then list the specific skills or knowledge required to produce each desired outcome. For example, if you want someone to open up your Spain sales office and produce $5 million in the first year, the specific skills might be:

- Proven fluency in Spanish, written and verbal

- The ability to attract, recruit, and retain top-producing sales people

- Telephone skills for securing meetings with C-level prospects

- General familiarity with telecom networking products

These would be the minimum required skills needed to produce the outcome you want. You might notice that you've deliberately omitted "must have intimate familiarity with gigabit networking products." It's appropriate to omit certain types of knowledge if you're willing to train the new hire in this area.

You don't want to have a laundry list of required skills and knowledge—just the mandatory items. The acid test is this: If the candidate is missing any of the items on your list of mandatory requirements you're certain it will be impossible for the candidate to succeed within your specified time frame.

That's the standard you want to aim for because it's clearly screens out people who can't get the job 100% done (even if they can get close). At the same time, it provides a high quality standard that still includes the broadest possible range of people who could get the job done.

Hiring Step #3:
Don't Hire the Best Candidate For the Role,
Hire the Candidate Who Is 100% Qualified

Once you have your list of mandatory skills and knowledge you hire only someone who meets all of the criteria. Because the list defines the minimum level of skills and knowledge required, if you hire someone who doesn't meet all of the criteria you've just guaranteed that the outcome you want will not be achieved.

A candidate is either 100% qualified or not. There is no middle ground. Don't hire the best available candidate (i.e., the "least worst" candidate); hire the person who meets **all** the mandatory requirements and is 100% qualified.

Hiring Step #4:
Look For Specific Proof of Skills Needed
to Deliver The Desired Outcome

When evaluating candidates, you want to use a "proof–based" approach. Look for three examples of how the candidate has demonstrated each specific skill, or knowledge area, that you require.

Continuing our previous example of looking for someone to open your Spain sales office, and referring to the mandatory requirements listed above, you would ask for up to three specific examples that prove the candidate's ability to in each mandatory area.

For proven language fluency you might discover that the candidate graduated from high school in Spain— that's probably sufficient.

For the requirement regarding attracting, recruiting, and retaining top-producing sales people you'd ask for specific examples that demonstrate that skill. Then you want to drill down into the specifics—much like how a criminal defense attorney cross-examines the prosecution's star witness.

You might ask these questions:

- Specifically, how many people did you manage when you were the head of Eastern Region Sales for Mega Corp?

- Of those people, how many did you personally hire?

- What was the specific revenue performance of your hires compared with the performance of hires by others?

- What was your individual sales representative quota?

- What percentage of your reps was above that quota?

- How many of the people you managed did you fire?

- On what basis did you decide when someone needed to be fired?

- What was the overall revenue performance of your group during the 12 months prior to your starting?

- What was the revenue performance during the final 12 months of your time running that region?

You'll notice that these are factual questions. All of them ask for a specific factual number. If the candidate legitimately performed well in his or her former (or current) position the candidate will have no problems answering these questions. Each question can have only one factually correct answer.

After you get one specific example proving the candidates ability in one skill or knowledge area, you want to repeat the process two more times. "Okay, give me another example of when you were able to attract, recruit, and retain top-producing sales people." Then, "Give me a third example."

While the transcript of such an interview seems adversarial, for a strong applicant it's an easy interview. All they have to do is remember what happened. They don't have to sell you on anything. They don't have to guess what answer you want to hear in response to some open-ended question.

In contrast for an applicant that's trying to "fake it," it becomes painfully obvious quickly if they're trying to "B.S." you. First of all nobody can lie that quickly and have all their lies tie together in a natural way. Also by asking for three examples that demonstrate each skill or knowledge area, you blow past any "prepared" answers the candidate had anticipated needing to give and you really get to see if their track record in an area runs deep. The bottom line is in this type of fact-based interview, it's really hard to hide.

These facts provide you with the objective data you need to reach a conclusion regarding the applicant's track record relative to a specific set of skills.

By using this rigorous and systematic process you will uncover enormous amounts of factual information. With this information you can make a fact-based assessment of the candidate's likelihood of producing the outcome you desire.

You'll notice that this process is much more rigorous than concluding that you "like the person." Sure, liking someone is important if you're going to be working with them; other than that, the only thing that matters is can the person produce results? It's all about results, results, results.

Hiring Tip #5:
Hire People With Upside Potential.

Another factor that's important to consider in fast-growing companies is the "upside potential" of a candidate. Upside potential is the estimation of how much more skilled and knowledgeable the candidate can become over time. In a nutshell, ask yourself if this candidate will continue to grow with more experience, or has the candidate already reached the ceiling of his or her career skills?

While this may seem subjective, the easiest way to empirically verify upside potential is to look at career trajectory. Has the person been in the same role for the past 20 years or has each role been more complicated, larger in scope, and more challenging? Has the person experienced diverse roles and situations that improved his or her skills?

In a company that's not growing this is not very important. However, in a fast-growing company you're going to need talent to drive more revenue growth engines. For this reason you deliberately want to favor 100%-qualified candidates who have the ability to grow into even bigger roles.

A corollary to this rule is: Hire the people you want to have running your companies three years from now and not the company you have today. This practice of "hiring for where you want to be—instead of where you are" approach is a good one to keep in mind.

Closing Thoughts

We started this section of the book talking about the three key areas that you, as the CEO, must focus on. We've covered managing the portfolio of revenue growth engines and managing talent. In the next chapter we'll discuss what you do with the talented hires once you have them on board—namely holding them accountable for producing results.

Key Ideas:

- The key to assembling the right executive team starts by knowing yourself. Stick to your exceptional talents, and hire others to cover your weaknesses

- "B" players focus on completing assigned activities, "A" players focus on delivering results

- Consider firing the bottom 10 to 20% of your employees every year to continually improve the overall quality of your team

- **Hiring Step #1:** Define results you want from a role before recruiting for it. Write a "results description" instead of a "job description"

- **Hiring Step #2:** Identify the key skills and knowledge areas needed to produce each result you require

- **Hiring Step #3:** Don't hire the best candidate (i.e., the least worst candidate), hire the candidate who is 100% qualified

- **Hiring Step #4:** Look for specific proof of skills and knowledge areas needed to deliver the outcomes you desire

- **Hiring Step #5:** Hire people with upside potential

CHAPTER 13

Accountability:
The Breakfast of Champions

The difference between a good idea and generating revenues from it comes from getting things done—in particular, getting revenue done. The key to getting revenue done in a fast-growing company is to hold your team accountable for producing results.

Execution and accountability are not sexy topics; it's not as cool as coming up with the killer business plan or business model. It's certainly not as fun as playing with the latest technologies. But it is where revenue gets produced. So, in that respect, it's absolutely essential.

Accountability is something you cannot—and must not—delegate. It is the key operating tool for managing a large company. The processes I'm going to show you work in multi-billion dollar companies as well as startup companies; they are scalable methods for managing people and are brutally effective for improving financial statement numbers.

In many companies people focus way too much on activities and nowhere near enough on financial results. A Vice President (VP) of Marketing might say, "We had a great quarter in the marketing department. We got 11 campaigns out the door, put on three events, and hosted three Webinars. It was a very busy quarter for us."

We don't care about people being busy; we only care about people being effective at increasing profitable revenues. A good quarter for marketing is one in which marketing efforts directly and collaboratively increased revenues. That's a good quarter.

Who really cares how many campaigns were launched, events thrown, Webinars given? The only thing that matters is the financial results from those campaigns, events, and Webinars. In other words, it's not about the marketing campaigns it's about the revenues produced from those marketing campaigns.

This mindset is also prevalent in other departments. Product development tend to think of a successful quarter as one in which a product was shipped. Once again, who cares if the product was shipped? The real question is, "Did you ship a product that customers ended up buying?" It's not about product launches; it's about products launched that sold. That's a big difference.

As CEO you must hold people accountable for results, not just activities. Something really interesting happens when you hold people accountable for results—they start focusing on the things that produce results.

Let's say you tell your VP of Engineering she will be held accountable for shipping a new product and making sure the product delivers $10 million in new product sales this quarter. The first thing she will do is object to the revenue target. She may proclaim it's unfair—she doesn't control the sales force. She would be right of course. But, you should hold her accountable anyways because it forces her to focus on the decisions and actions she does control that contribute to the desired results.

In response to the protest you could reply, "Well then, I strongly suggest that you talk to the VP of Sales. You need to make sure that his sales force has what it needs to sell your product."

Let's say the team collectively misses the goal—the product shipped on time but sales fell short of the $10 million goal. The VP of Engineering is now frustrated that she's taking flack from you for delivering a product that didn't sell. The VP now knows you're serious about this results thing.

She pulls in a few of her top folks and says, "Okay, listen. The CEO is only giving us gold stars this quarter if we ship a product that sells. I don't know if the sales people are screwing up or if customers really don't want to buy what we're shipping, but this is not going to happen again. I want you guys to buddy up with a few of the top sales people in the field and figure out what the heck's going on. I'm tagging along because this crap is not happening on my watch."

Now, typically, one of several things will happen in this type of situation. The next product release will be much more sellable, or the real underlying problem will surface (which is typically that someone, somewhere, isn't doing their job).

When you hold people accountable for results, hidden problems (especially people who aren't performing) surface much more quickly. This is good because the problems can then be resolved that much faster.

The Accountability System

Here's a specific process that I like using to keep an executive team accountable. Let me describe the basic process and then talk about making some adjustments depending on how fast your company is growing (generally, the faster you're growing, the more frequently you need to employ the accountability process).

Step #1:
Define the Revenue Goal

The first step of this process is to define your company's overall revenue objective and timeframe. This is typically the monthly, quarterly, and fiscal year revenue targets. Most companies do this, so this is not that big a deal.

Step #2:
Identify the Revenue Contribution Expected From Each Revenue Growth Engine

In this step you want to measure revenues expected from each revenue source. Typically, your revenue sources will consist of several existing revenue streams and several revenue growth engine projects.

Total the revenue contribution from each individual source and this should equal or exceed the revenue target for the company.

If a company screws up this process, it usually happens in the next few steps. Once you have revenue expectations identified by revenue source, you need to critically assess the action plans behind each revenue sources. The types of questions that need to be asked are also similar in style to a lawyer cross-examining a hostile witness. These questions might include:

- What makes you think you can achieve this revenue target?

- How will you get more customers? What information do you have that suggest these plans will work?

- Do you have your key people in place yet?

- What are the major risks and uncertainties in your plan? What are your contingency plans?

- Your schedule looks awfully aggressively, maybe even unrealistic. Is every item in your plan on schedule so far?

There are two big lessons here. The first is you get the big revenue growth numbers by focusing on the individual revenue growth engines. This is where the money is made. The second lesson is to realize that you need to determine if the revenue from a particular growth engine is likely to materialize before you reach your deadline—while you still have time to make adjustments. You do this by attempting to poke holes in the action plan and results to date.

If you can't find a flaw in the plan, then your confidence level that a particular growth engine will be able to meet its revenue target will be high. If you discover an action plan is horribly flawed or unrealistic, then you know you need to make some changes to the plan, the team, or both.

Step #3:
Assign One Person Per Revenue Source
to Deliver the Expected Revenues

Each revenue source be assigned to a single person who will "commit" to delivering the expected outcome. For revenue streams that truly require cross-functional effort you still want to have one key person who is the lead. Each growth engine leader is held responsible for coming up with the action plan and programs needed to produce the desired financial results. This plan is then approved, and continually monitored, at your monthly operations review meetings.

Step #4:
Use a Monthly Operations Review
to Enforce Accountability

The monthly operations review meeting is an important mechanism for managing a fast-growing company. This meeting is a forum for making decisions about revenue growth portfolio additions, subtractions, modifications, and re-sequencing activities. It is the place where talent is assigned, or re-assigned, to lead revenue growth engine opportunities.

The purpose of the meeting is to determine what needs to be done, who is going to get it done, and to verify that assigned outcomes are achieved.

At each meeting the department head presents an update of department operations, and each growth engine leader (some of whom may also be department heads) provides an update on the revenue growth engine projects they lead. This update should include the following:

- A reminder of the objectives committed to at the last meeting and an update on results achieved relative to the objectives

- A review of key operating and financial performance metrics

- The identification of any current or anticipated obstacles that require a cross-functional audience to resolve

- A description of the objectives that the leader commits to achieving by the next meeting (or other standard time period)

In addition to reviewing the progress of existing revenue growth engine, you should have key leaders present new growth engines opportunities. You want to use the opportunity to debate, approve or decline proposed growth engine opportunities.

Operations Review Frequency

For many companies, a monthly operations review is sufficient. In some very early-stage companies, or companies that are growing quickly, you'll want to hold these rigorous meetings more frequently.

You can also conduct shorter "check-in" meetings or teleconferences on a more frequent basis, such as during a weekly senior staff meeting. These "check-in" meetings are for information sharing and for surfacing obstacles that require cross-functional involvement, discussion, or decision-making.

While the short check-in meetings are useful, you'll want to save the "deep dive" discussions for the operations review meeting.

A Scalable Management Process For the CEO

This accountability process is highly scalable, which means it can be used to run companies of $1 million a year, $10 million a year, $100 million a year, or even a $1 billion a year. I've personally participated in these kinds of meetings at companies of all levels and can assure you: The core process works, with only minor adjustments needed to accommodate the size of the company.

Key Ideas:

- A CEO must hold people accountable for results, not activities

- Use a four-step "Accountability System" to ensure that the right things are getting done on time

- **Step #1:** Define the revenue goal for the company as a whole

- **Step #2:** Identify the revenue contribution expected from each revenue growth engine

- **Step #3:** Assign one person per revenue source to deliver the expected revenues

- **Step #4:** Use a monthly operations review to enforce accountability

Part IV:
How to Get Started

CHAPTER 14

3 Strategies To Jump Start Growth

In this chapter I'll be talking about the three strategies for jump starting growth and getting on the path to extreme revenue growth.

Strategy #1:
Extreme Revenue Growth Starts with
"Thinking Bigger"

My clients love me and my clients hate me. They love me because I show them the path to more revenues and give them the specific processes they need to use to get there. (Incidentally, the most important word in that last sentence is process. Extreme revenue growth is as much about the "big idea" as it is about the "nuts and bolts" tasks you need to do to turn a "big idea" into big revenue.) But at the same time I deliberately do things that cause them to "hate" me.

They hate me because I routinely push them to "think bigger"—much bigger than they're accustomed to thinking and way beyond their comfort zones. I suppose it's more accurate to say that my clients hate feeling uncomfortable—and with me they're always outside their comfort zone.

I push them to think bigger, I push them to act faster, and I push them to be more decisive. Basically, I push them constantly. I had one client who once asked me, "Victor, don't you ever let up?" My reply was, "Well, it wasn't my idea to add another $900 million in revenue in the next 10 years—that was *your* idea."

A Personal Story About Thinking Bigger

Let me share with you why I push my clients to think bigger. It's something I learned from my high school football coach who was this tough-as-nails former NFL player. You wouldn't believe how much this guy wanted to win. He would run stamina drills until someone vomited. He would make us do 25 push-ups as a team but would suddenly pretend to forget how to count. He would start off like this: "Push-up #1, #2, #3, #3, #3, #3, #4…" His theory was, "You never know where your physical limits really are, so I'm going to prove to you that your physical limits are way beyond where you think they are."

He was right. After 4 years of that stuff every single day I was routinely running full speed, head to head, against guys up to 70 pounds heavier and 12 inches taller than me—fully expecting to knock the other guy on his rear. And I often did. The reason? Because by the time that coach was done with me I had no mental barriers against what was physically possible—which wasn't true for the other, bigger guy.

This coach knew that I would never play at my physical capacity when my self-imposed mental boundaries were so limiting. His approach worked.

During my senior year I was co-captain of the team. We won a California state championship, and, several years later, one of our players went on to win the Heisman Trophy—the award granted to the #1 college football player in the country.

On a personal note, he pushed me well beyond what I thought a little, geeky super-nerd from Southern California could ever do—and I've never been the same since. So, I constantly insist that my CEO clients "think bigger."

Thinking Bigger For Legitimate Reasons

Extreme revenue growth, while simple, is not easy. Every decision, every action—everything—has to be a push for growth. This is especially true when it comes to thinking "bigger."

With most of my clients I take a look at the assets they have to work with, and I see much greater revenue potential than they see. While my clients know their own business in great depth, I focus on developing a broader perspective. Through my client work, my own experiences, and on-going research, I keep tabs on what hundreds of companies, in dozens of industries, are doing to achieve extraordinary revenue growth.

This extensive background and awareness of how companies have cleverly gotten more value out of a particular type of asset, has come in handy. It allows me to show my clients ways of extracting more value out of a given set of customers, products, services, distribution channels, and people than they themselves typically see.

For the client who comes to me with a $100 million a year business I can often see how they could be a $500 million a year business, even though the CEO has difficulty seeing how to get past $150 million.

For the startup with $1 million in sales, sometimes I can see how they can get to $5 million in the next 18 months (with extremely radical changes, mind you, but I can see how it can be done).

For the company with $20 million I can see how they could reach $100 million in the next two years (several major things would all have to go exactly right and be done with a massive sense of urgency, but it would possible).

Sometimes such extreme growth might involve a series of five or six major "strategic moves" over a period of years—but the key to achieving such growth starts with "thinking bigger."

Here's another reason why thinking bigger is so important:

You Can't Grow Big While Thinking Small

When I first started advising clients on extreme revenue growth I focused primarily on the strategic and tactical issues inside the company. But, I discovered something unexpected that has changed my approach. I discovered that you can't grow big if your tendency is to think small.

If your goal is to grow 50% in the next two years you will automatically filter out any opportunity to grow 500% in the next two years—for reasons revealed through the numerous client examples I'll share with you in a moment. I've come to the conclusion that the single biggest bottleneck to revenue growth isn't products, distribution, people, or processes—it's a CEO who "thinks too small."

So my approach today focuses on both the nuts and bolts of the client's business and the growth expectations of its leader. When I see a 500% growth opportunity and the client sees only a 50% opportunity, here's what I do: I give a logical explanation for why I see the revenue growth potential that I do—then I pretty much harass the client until he or she starts thinking bigger. Here's an example:

Case Study #1:
The CEO Who Thought "Too Small"

One company owner asked me to consider taking his company on as a client (the company had experienced three years of flat growth). I looked at the business and saw that, despite the flat revenues, there was enormous untapped potential, so I took him on as a client.

During our first phone call he mentioned that he was looking to grow by 50% in the current year, which would have been a huge relief for him after three years of flat revenues. Based on what I'd seen of his business, I told him I thought he was aiming way too low.

Instead of 50% growth in the first year I was thinking more along the lines of 500% growth in the first year. That kind of growth would not be easy—much would have to go right, and extremely quickly, but I thought it was possible and worth aiming for. I have to laugh because the guy almost passed out.

But I kept pounding on his "small thinking," over and over again. I was, frankly, relentless. I yelled at him constantly, "Stop aiming for $40k deals! Work your way up to $800k deals!" (He almost passed out again.)

"What do you mean $800k deals? Victor, are you CRAZY?"

"No, I'm not crazy. Look, don't you see that you're solving a $100 million problem for your customer? I don't care if you're used to a $40k fee, but an $800k fee to solve a $100 million problem is very reasonable."

Logically, he understood, but he was just not used to thinking big. I pushed him constantly to think bigger. I kept throwing out big numbers—numbers larger than he was used to considering—to de-sensitize his mind to big numbers and to increase his comfort level with them.

I admit it; I used pure psychological warfare to get him to think bigger. I did it because: First, it was in his best interest, and second, while extreme revenue growth is simple, it is not easy, and he had to think bigger—much bigger—if he wanted to grow his company.

The harassment worked. Just 30 days later his company landed the single biggest deal in company history—400% bigger than the previous year's average deal. Sixty days later his company repeated the feat, landing another deal of equal size.

In the first year under my advisement (okay, harassment) he ended the year with sales 245% higher than the previous year. Not what I had in mind for him, but reasonable.

Did we use many of the extreme growth techniques mentioned in this book? Yes. Would any of the techniques have been effective if he had kept on thinking small? No. That's why thinking bigger is so important; if you don't, the rest, frankly, doesn't matter.

Strategy #2:
Isolate, Focus on, and Fix the Biggest Bottleneck

The three phases of extreme revenue growth are: creating it, managing it, and sustaining it. One of the keys to getting started is to have a clear, honest, and frank sense of which phase is actually holding back your growth the most.

For some companies this is obvious. If you're starting a new company, or a new division of an existing company, the top priority is creating more growth. But, in other situations it's not always so clear.

If your company generates $200 million in sales but your team is distracted by a lot of "fires" that keep popping up unexpectedly, do you have a problem sustaining growth or managing the growth you already generated? Is the problem that you don't know how to grow or is the problem that your systems are so poor that "fires" keep popping up and distracted your team from growing the business?

The Two Most Common, but Not Obvious, Growth Bottlenecks

The most common problems my new clients suffer from without realizing it stem from the issues related to "managing growth" (process standardization, the 10 times test, and systems). In these cases the client initially focuses incorrectly on the more visible symptom (I need more revenues), rather than the "behind the scenes" problems that underlie the symptoms.

It's difficult to get a company to surge forward and grow when it continually leaves behind an operational mess and tons of fires that need to be put out.

It's somewhat like the foundation of a skyscraper. A skyscraper's foundation is boring, mostly because nobody sees it. But if you don't build the foundation correctly the rest of the skyscraper falls apart. If the top floor of the building is unstable don't go looking for the problem up there—look down at the foundation.

The same is true with your systems and procedures. It's important to take a hard look at your business to see where the weaknesses actually are. System-related problems exist in all the companies I've worked with, whether they be $5 million, $150 million, or $300 million a year companies.

Just because your company is big doesn't mean you have all your systems in order—because with size comes new types of systems that weren't necessary when your company was smaller.

The second most commonly overlooked bottleneck to growth comes from people-related problems. Often, a CEO will have the right growth engine in mind, know precisely how to capture a tightly focused market segment, but somehow the results don't materialize. While there are many places in which to look for problems, the one that often gets overlooked is the area of people issues—notably, a lack of disciplined processes or systems for recruiting people, managing them, and holding them accountable for results.

To Fix the Bottleneck, You Must First Isolate It

In my client work I routinely direct clients away from the highly visible "symptoms" in their business (which, by the way, is why they contacted me) to the hidden problems that cause the symptoms. Unfortunately, this is not an easy process for the client company to go through. Even though the clients gets good results, the process is an uncomfortable one to under take.

Here are a few case studies that illustrate this point:

Case Study #2:
The Revenue Growth Ceiling Caused
by a Hidden People Problem

One of my startup clients runs an Internet company that provides health-related products and services to consumers. I had worked with him briefly three years ago to "create growth," which resulted in monthly revenues growing by over 150% in the first four months. At the time he had a strong growth market, well-regarded products, and a good marketing program. But his primary bottleneck came from the lack of sufficient distribution. I showed him how to "multiply" his distribution efforts quickly. Over the following 18 months he continued to grow, posting a 400% growth over a two-year period.

However, during the 12 months following this 400% growth period his company revenues slammed into a revenue ceiling. He was frustrated because he had good products, happy customers, and decent distribution in a market that itself was growing quite rapidly. Yet, for some reason, the revenue growth was no longer there.

Within about two hours of getting the latest update on his business and the many "symptoms" he was concerned about, I found the underlying "problem" that was causing his headaches: His team.

What he thought was a growth problem was really a people problem. He had the wrong people on his team, a poor process for hiring the right people, and no process for getting rid of people who were not performing.

Together we created a 90-day plan to replace 80% of his upper management. Yes, 80% of his team had to go. (You can see why my clients are in a constant state of discomfort when I get involved.)

This, of course, was a fairly dramatic shift. So we broke the transition into a few steps. First, we focused on replacing the 40% of his team causing serious problems at the time, which would create openings and funding to get a few "A" players into critical positions.

Once we had the new hires on board the plan was to upgrade the remaining 40%—the part of the team that wasn't doing any harm at the time but clearly couldn't go the distance.

So, even though he thought his problem was revenue growth, with my guidance, he quickly realized that his real problem was a people problem. Keep in mind that this was in the context of figuring out how to grow his company another 500% in the next two or three years. The bottom line was that his team was sufficient to get him to where he was but not where he wanted to go.

Achieving extreme revenue growth often requires significant changes. The challenge is to recognize that sometimes the underlying causes of problems aren't always obvious. You have to do some digging to isolate the real problem.

Case Study #3:
The Company's Customer Service Operations Couldn't Keep Up with Sales

Another client came to me seeking guidance for how to sustain his company's extreme revenue growth. For the three years prior to my advising him his company experienced three years of flat revenues. With my guidance, and a fantastic job of execution on his part, he generated 10 times growth over the next three years.

In one of our more recent conversations he indicated his interest in making sure he was doing the right things to sustain that growth rate.

Earlier in this book I mentioned two key concepts: The first was that bottlenecks constrain the revenue growth of your company, and the second was that once you remove one bottleneck another will make itself visible elsewhere in your company. This was certainly the case with this client. As you'll see, his number one issue has evolved substantially.

During the three years I worked with this client I advised him on these key issues and decisions:

1) The company left a market that didn't value his company's unique competitive advantages (the client had a good company, a good team, and good skills—but they were being applied to a market where his company simply could not win—so I got him out of that market).

2) He shifted his team and company to higher revenue potential opportunities. Revenues grew significantly—but he quickly realized that he had no sustainable competitive advantage, so the sustainability of revenues was in question.

3) The company transitioned from highly profitable revenue opportunities that had no sustainable competitive advantage to an equally attractive opportunity that could be sustained over the long term. He ended up killing a highly profitable, but ultimately unsustainable, revenue growth engine to put resources into one with stronger long-term potential. It worked. His company revenues ended up growing faster than his team's ability to handle clients.

4) He ended up standardizing his operations. He focused his team on creating client-service

procedures, standards, and systems that enabled his staff to handle client service with little involvement from him personally. This freed him from spending 10% of his time each week on strategic partnerships (his number one distribution channel) to 80% of his time each week—which, not surprisingly, significantly increased revenues.

With this additional time focused on signing strategic partnerships, he's now looking at an opportunity to grow revenues by 5 times over the next two years. It's already clear that his newly standardized systems can't possible scale up to those revenue levels. His systems, while documented, are too labor intensive to handle future growth.

5) I now have him focused on re-designing his operations systems to make them scalable by removing the key bottlenecks. Rather than offering each client a fully customized service, he's looking to off a set of standardized packages. He's considering the use of a third-party flex-staffing firm and creating long-term contracts with key vendors.

6) Once he gets his client service processes to be more scalable, I'll be directing his focus on creating standardized systems for cutting strategic partnership deals. I'd like him to double, if not triple, his staff in that area (but there's no point in doing that just yet because he knows he can't operationally take on that many more clients).

So that's where the company is today. You'll notice that it's a long way from where he started. The number one issue at each stage of growth was dramatically different from the one preceding it.

He exited markets, entered them, focused on shoring up sustainable competitive advantages, established systems in his client-service operations, focused on scalability of his key systems, and will soon be looking to increase his staffing in partnerships by 2 to 3 times.

I'm certain that I'll be discussing completely different issues with this client a year from now because that's the nature of the extreme growth game—wildly different issues at different phases of growth.

Having developed a fair amount of expertise in this area I suggest you be prepared for a wide range of issues related to extreme growth. It's a common trait of companies that grow quickly, and such dramatic "growing pains"-related changes should be anticipated, expected, and welcomed.

Strategy #3:
Start by Exploiting the Under-Utilized Asset

One of the best places to start on the path to extreme revenue growth is to unlock the stored value in an under-utilized asset. It's the surest way to get a quick initial surge of revenues. It's something I've done with every client I've advised over the past few years. Let me explain what I mean.

I interviewed and evaluated in great detail every long-term client I currently work with before taking them on. I've often analyzed gross margins, technology platforms, key accounts, growth trajectories, key intellectual property assets, key relationships, and countless other details—before taking a company on as a long-term client.

Let me share with you why I have such a rigorous prospective client evaluation process. It's quite revealing.

First, you need to know that, on a personal level, I like working with companies that have extreme revenue growth potential. It's a lot of fun, with no shortage of problems and challenges to overcome. My short attention span requires more, more, and more. I need more problems, more challenges, and more issues to advise my clients in tackling. For me, no growth equals no fun.

Second, my track record with extreme revenue growth is pretty good. Eighty percent of the CEOs I advise for six months or longer end up at least doubling their revenues if they're a startup, less if they're a more mature company. Frankly, this track record has as much to do with my expertise as it does with my only taking on clients that have the key ingredients to achieve this kind of growth. If a prospective client doesn't have the assets in place to achieve extreme revenue growth I simply decline to take them on.

Okay, so why bother going through all this work on my part before taking on a long-term client? Here's why I do it and, more importantly, why it's relevant to you in your quest for extreme revenue growth.

The secret to my track record is that I only work with clients that have a valuable, under-utilized asset. That's the big secret. It really doesn't matter what their current revenues are. Some prospective clients come to me when their revenues are flat. Others approach me when they are already growing at 50% or more per year. In every case I look for an under-utilized asset that can be exploited quickly on the client's behalf—that brings an initial surge of extreme revenue growth. I do this because the initial revenue surge gets the client interested enough to take on the much more difficult task of sustaining extreme revenue growth.

Let me give you an example.

Case Study #4:
A $300 Million a Year Distribution Channel
Stuck in a $3 Million a Year Company

I was chatting with the CEO of a manufacturing company with $3 million a year in revenues. The company was plugging along, trying to crank out more and more products. The challenge for them was that they sold primarily to large accounts that were slow to pay invoices. These clients took 3 to 4 months to pay its invoices. Meanwhile this manufacturing company had to pay its bills within 30 days. As a result, their cash flow problems grew worse every time revenues increase.

So what was the hidden, untapped asset for this company that I noticed? Distribution.

Despite being small this company had access to ALL the major Fortune 500 buyers in their market. I'm not talking about a few; I'm talking about literally ALL of them. I was quite surprised, because this kind of distribution power is highly unusual for a company with only $3 million in sales. It's a level of distribution that I would have expected to see in a company with $300 million in sales.

So, here's a situation in which the company's cash flow model was constrained to $3 million a year. The ability to produce products was also constrained to about $3 million a year. But, here was this unpolished gem of a distribution channel capable of producing $300 million a year—stuck in a company doing only $3 million in sales.

The thing is, the CEO of the company didn't see it. He was (not surprisingly) really focused on the cash flow crunch and establishing new lines of credit to fund his working capital.

By the way, the overlooked "extreme revenue growth engine" opportunity that I identified for him was for his company to become the de facto sales force for the rest of the manufacturers in his industry. He had CEOs of hundreds of companies in his industry with related (but non-competitive) products that would have donated a kidney to get access to the kind of distribution this CEO was taking for granted.

By leveraging this un-tapped, highly desirable asset, he could pass-thru the accounts receivables terms from the Fortune 500 buyers all the way through to these other manufacturers. This would solve his cash flow problem and remove working capital as a constraint to growth.

Second, this wholesaling opportunity would leverage the product design and manufacturing capacity of his entire industry—removing the $3 million per year capacity constraints his own company had in manufacturing and product design.

This process systematically removes all the major bottlenecks that prevent his "hidden gem" $300 million a year capable distribution channel from being fully utilized.

The CEO never thought of this opportunity before I brought it to his attention. He was so ingrained in the mindset of "I'm a CEO of a manufacturing company" that he never considered something bigger and broader. Sometimes a fresh, outside perspective is all it takes to open the door to extreme revenue growth.

Hopefully, you can see from this case study the value of looking for the under-utilized asset that can be exploited often with fabulous results. Oftentimes, there's enormous value sitting inside your company untapped. Unlocking the value in an under-utilized asset is one of my favorite places to start.

Key Ideas:

- There are three strategies for jump starting growth for fast, immediate surges in revenues

- **Strategy #1:** Think Bigger

- **Strategy #2:** Isolate, focus on, and fix the biggest revenue growth bottleneck

- **Strategy #3:** Start by exploiting the under-utilized asset

CHAPTER 15

Additional Resources

I hope you've found this book to be a useful resource and inspiration for starting your company's journey toward extreme revenue growth.

I do have one favor to ask. I'd like to know what you thought of the book and would welcome any suggestions you may have. I'd really appreciate it if you could send a quick email to feedback@victorcheng.com.

I do read all feedback personally. And I plan to use your feedback to improve the next edition of this book and to refine my plans for future books and resources. (And yes, if you've been paying close attention, this is a variation of the "suggest a feature" feature I recommend you include in all of your products. I do practice what I preach!)

One of the big themes I've tried to convey is that extreme growth doesn't come from a one-time project or implementing one new idea. Instead, achieving consistently aggressive revenue growth is an ongoing process—working on the fundamentals of building a bigger business day in, day out, on a consistent basis.

To assist you in achieving your goals, I'd like to offer some additional resources that you may find helpful.

Resource #1: Email Newsletter

The first resource is my email newsletter. As an author, one of the ongoing frustrations is the minute you're done writing a book, you immediately wish you could add something else—a new tool, an interesting case example, or new ideas on the book's topic. Fortunately, with my email newsletter I'm able to share with you all my current and up-to-date thinking on achieving extreme revenue growth in your company.

I publish my newsletter only when I have something useful to offer. Think of each issue as the equivalent of a mini-chapter of this book and you'll have an idea of what I strive for with each issue.

To receive my latest updates and tips on achieving extreme growth in your company, visit the following website:

www.VictorCheng.com/extreme

Resource #2: Consulting Services

I do work with companies on an individualized consulting basis, serving as a strategic advisor or in some cases as a board member. If you'd like to explore the possibility of working together, feel free to contact me using the contact information below.

Closing Remarks

Finally, I want to wish you the best of luck in achieving extreme revenue growth in your company.

Author Contact Information

Website:	www.VictorCheng.com
eNewsletter:	www.VictorCheng.com/extreme
Email:	victor@victorcheng.com
Phone:	800-460-2164 x115

CPSIA information can be obtained
at www.ICGtesting.com
Printed in the USA
FSHW010357010320

9 780984 183517